Emanuele Schmidt

Key performance indicators for retail

The story behind the figures

THE STORE MANAGER'S HANDBOOK

Ledizioni

© Edizioni Ledizioni LediPublishing
Via Alamanni 11 Milano
http://www.ledizioni.it
e-mail: info@ledizioni.it

First edition: december 2015

EMANUELE SCHMIDT, *Key performance indicator for retail*

Cover designed by Roberta Maddaloni
Printed in Italy
ISBN 978-88-6705-413-8

CONTENTS

It's a misty autumn morning, and I'm starting to write this book about key performance indicators for retail. My goal is to help whoever reads it to:

Understand how the store is doing;
And make the "right" decisions.

I'm wondering who my readers will be. If I can imagine who you are, dear reader, I think it will be easier to write.

Maybe you have just been *promoted to be a store manager*: I picture you as an adept, successful salesperson who is passionate about the products and the art of selling. Your bosses have offered you the promotion and you've accepted it. 'What new things will I need to know? What will I have to do differently? What will it be like to manage people? And the figures … I don't have a good head for maths!' These might be some of things going through your head now.

Or maybe you are already a *store manager* in a chain of mono- or multi-brand stores; you are already well acquainted with the role but are unsure about a couple of aspects and would like to learn more. Perhaps your company is asking you to perform new tasks, such as devising and managing local marketing initiatives; or you reckon your store could do more and/or better, or maybe you are worried about the seemingly high turnover of staff that you cannot explain. Or maybe you just feel like a novice who has been thrown in at the deep end because your company never gave you the opportunity to go on any training courses.

You might be an *"apprentice"* in a distribution chain: perhaps you are a school leaver or have just graduated and this is your first "proper" job (if we leave aside your previous experiences as a waiter, night-time shelf-stacker in a supermarket, lifeguard, babysitter, seasonal postal worker and sales assistant in a city-centre shop over

Christmas). Your first months in the position involved lessons as well as on-the-job training in different stores and your ultimate goal is to be a store manager. You've got everything to learn!

And what if you are an *entrepreneur*? You have already owned one or more stores ... for years! In this case, I could probably ask you to write this book: you know your store's results inside outside, certainly better than I do! Or maybe not? Are you part of the club of people who want a better understanding, who want to comprehend the dynamics of some indicators that you wouldn't normally use; or something hasn't been quite right for a while now and you want to know what is it: who knows, maybe this book might give you a helping hand ...

You could be the *son or daughter of an entrepreneur*. Your parents have a store and are insisting that you join the family business. You have already worked a couple of summers for them. Having your parents as your boss isn't the easiest thing in this world, but the idea of running your own store is starting to look quite tempting. Maybe not? You don't like it but you want to consider your options before closing that door forever. Perhaps you reckon many things could be done differently, maybe you think your parents are a bit too "traditional" and are missing opportunities. Now if only they would just let you get on with it ...

Maybe you are a *retail manager* or a *sales manager*. You bought this book to see if you could use it in staff training. Or you are a *training manager* and want to hand out this book during your courses on the economics of retail. You are a *trainer* who teaches these or similar subjects and want a better idea. You are a high school teacher, a university researcher ...

So many potential readers! There again, there are millions of stores around the world: it's not surprising that there are so many people that might be interested in what I have to say.

I'm galvanised by the outcome of my thought experiment; it has fuelled my motivation to write and my desire to offer a book about how to interpret key performance indicators for retail that is straightforward, fun, and incisive.

This book is designed to be easy to read, practical and to the point and has been written for people who are in charge of managing a store.

I know that there are many differences in retail: the specific nature of the products, the size of the stores, the decision to sell multiple brands or just one, the size of the organisation … and the list goes on. However, I firmly believe that managing stores is a profession based on a number of cross-disciplinary skills that are always valid irrespective of any specific commercial formula. One of these general skills is to throughly understand store's results and this is the goal of this book.

INTRODUCTION

HOW TO USE KEY PERFORMANCE INDICATORS

I was chatting with a client a few months ago:

Client: "My store managers need to learn how to manage the store's performance indicators!"

Me: "Managing performance indicators is impossible."

Client: ???!!! (his expression was a combination of puzzled and vexed).

Me: "I'll give you an example. I'm driving my car and the speedometer reads 130 kilometres per hour. The road sign on the side of the motorway (the round white sign with a red border) unequivocally states that the maximum speed limit is 100 kilometres per hour. What do I need to do to make things right? Open the speedometer and adjust the needle, or take my foot off the accelerator?"

Client: "Now I see what you're getting at ..."

Me: "The point is to be clear about what we mean by *manage*. If an indicator is a number that represents the result of somebody's work, the only way to *directly* manage it is to manipulate it (for example, take a report and alter the figures). But if we use manage to mean *improve the results*, then yes indicators are useful: we can use them to make decisions."

Client: "So, you're telling me that you can't directly manage results, or even the figures that represent them. But you can make decisions with varying degrees of efficacy that lead to results with varying degrees of success. And in turn these results depend on how these decisions are implemented …"

Me: "… and on the market's response to them: how customers respond, which countermoves your competitors make. A good decision that doesn't have any positive effects is not a good decision."

When we talk about "managing" key performance indicators for retail, we refer to the **decision-making cycle**, which is a manager's main responsibility. So we are actually talking about a logical series of steps that is continuously repeated:

1. **I measure the results;**
2. **I understand what has happened and why it has happened;**
3. **I set a goal;**
4. **I identify actions that should help me to achieve that goal;**
5. **I implement them;**
6. **I wait for the time it takes for the market to respond;**
7. **I measure the results again.**

This series of steps can be illustrated with a cycle:

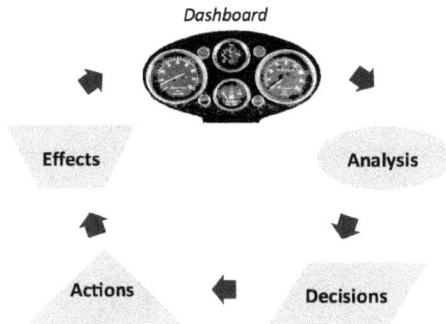

Dashboard

Effects

Analysis

Actions

Decisions

Let's look at an example set in an apparel store. The sales KPI tells me that the results for the "men's socks" category are lower than you would reasonably expect to see. The store manager *analyses* the situation and discovers that:
- Many of the products are not displayed on the shelf;
- The products are in disarray and the price tags cannot be easily read;
- The display shelf is dirty;
- The prices are on average 8% higher than those of the nearest competitors;
- Many of the socks that should be displayed on the shelf are actually buried under other boxes in the stockroom.

Based on these discoveries, the manager sets a *goal* to increase sales and establishes some *actions* that are relevant to this goal: clean the shelf, fill it with the missing products, and organise the price tags. He sets a sales assistant the task of keeping the shelf tidy and well stocked. He decides not to lower the prices for the time being, preferring to wait and see what *effects* his actions will have, i.e. how will the customer respond to a better stocked and more attractive shelf. After that, the cycle begins all over again ...

I have deliberately chosen a straightforward example: it represents the essence of the manager's reasoning process. The problems that need to be resolved are often more complicated and the solution is not as simple or predictable, but the core logic is the same.

The figures, the KPIs, are normally documented in a series of reports, or in a software application that offers a real-time snapshot of the situation. Some call this the "dashboard" because, just like in a car, it provides all the most important information so you can keep an eye on how things are progressing. Every company has its own system of indicators and its ways of making these available.

Reports are always written in the past tense. They contain information about what has already happened and can no longer be altered. When reports contain information about the future (the budget), they deal with goals that an organisation has set itself, and thereby talk about forecasts, expectations, standards or "wishes": measurement is always based on what has already happened.

The dashboard is a container for various types of economic performance indicators. Just like in a car, there shouldn't be too many (otherwise you risk getting bogged down in details without knowing how to use them), nor should there be too few (otherwise you will lack the information you need to make decisions). The dashboard should contain the "right" number of the "right" indicators. Well, that's easy to say but …

Which are the key performance indicators for retail?

When I was setting out the contents for this book, I decided to follow the customer through his or her *shopping experience*: the customer enters the store, buys, leaves, expresses an opinion (if someone asks), and returns. There are precise indicators for each one of these steps. The first 12 chapters follow the customers through their shopping experience.

Chapters 13 to 16 introduce the indicators that measure "internal" aspects which are less noticeable to the customers. Finally, chapter 17 offers a review: the profit and loss statement.

Given that the same indicator may have different names in different companies I have used a standard term for each indicator. These are the indicators that I will be looking at (in order of "appearance").

Footfall
Number of transactions
Conversion rate
Net sales
Sales per square meter
Average sale per transaction
Average selling price

Units per transaction

Sales per category

Number of categories per transaction

Penetration

Margins

Percentage of revenue from promotions

Markdowns

Loyalty / Percentage of revenue from return customers

Customer Satisfaction

Mystery Shopper

Stock rotation / Inventory turnover

Stock coverage

Damaged items

Shrinkage

Returns

Personnel costs

Sales per hour / per FTE

Direct operating costs

A READER'S GUIDE

Each chapter looks at one or more indicators, and provides the following information:

1. A definition;
2. What the indicator measures;
3. How to calculate the indicator;
4. Which variables influence the indicator;
5. The store manager's actionable levers for changing the indicator.

I can't give you information about where to find the indicator (i.e. how to find it) because I am writing for people who work in different types of companies and perform different roles. I have worked around this by leaving a space where you can make notes and jot down what you need to do to find the information.

Providing an even more important piece of information will also be tricky: how to assess whether a certain result is positive or negative. When we pick up the results of a blood test there is a reference range (usually with two values) next to each parameter that helps us to immediately understand if things are alright, even though we are not experts.

So why can't I give you parameters like these?

For the same reason as before: this book has been written for the people who work in a range of different sectors. These sectors have different commercial dynamics and deal with different product categories. So, providing a universal benchmark is practically impossible. Once again I have left a blank space so you can make a note of your company's standards or objectives; where possible I will give some examples about how the benchmark may vary according to the type of store or products we are dealing with.

There are no hard and fast rules about how to read this book: you can work your way through, read the chapters in a different order, skip chapters or just read about the indicators that interest you and your situation. If you want, you can even skip the exercises (please see the next paragraph for more about this).

THE TWIN STORE EXERCISE

For each indicator I have prepared an exercise, which is known as "the twin store exercise".

Imagine two stores that are practically identical: they are the same size, selling the same product category, operates in similar settings, and they target the same customer segments. What they sell is not important but they sell the same products to very similar customers. I won't even tell you which currency they use as that is not essential to understanding our exercise.

At the beginning of each chapter I will tell you the results achieved by the two twin stores and I'll ask a simple question: why?

I'll ask you to come up with hypothesis about the possible reasons why these two stores produce different results. Each time I will also give you a benchmark, which may be the result from the previous period, a standard or a company goal, the company average, or the best performer's results. This will provide some additional information to help you work out your hypothesis.

And then I will ask another really simple question: what would you do? I'll ask you to put yourself in the store manager's shoes and decide which decisions he/she needs to make.

There are some possible reasons and answers in the appendix: try comparing them with your own.

The first indicator we meet on our journey into the world of KPIs is "**footfall**". Not all stores uses this indicator but it is very useful nevertheless. So what is footfall?

A store's footfall is the number of people who enter that store, for whatever reason, during a given period of time (an hour, day, week, month, or year).

What does this indicator measure?

Footfall measures how attractive **a store is to shoppers**, i.e. its ability to convince customers to choose the store and come through the door. The more people that enter the store, the higher the probability that the store has characteristics considered positive by its potential customers.

Footfall also allows us to learn more about the customers' buying habits: which days of the week attract more customers? Which are the quiet days? Which times of the day do customers prefer? So, footfall gives us information that is vital for planning the staff's shifts.

How do I calculate this indicator?

To measure footfall, we just need to **count how many people come through the door**. We usually use automatic systems to do this, which statistically adjust the figures. For example, some systems adjust down by a small percentage (between 3% and 6%) to deduct the number of times staff members enter and exit the store.

Footfall can be counted manually in stores that have a limited number of customers (for example, boutiques or furniture stores in which sales assistants accompany the customer) and someone who always monitors the entrance.

What is this indicator called in your business?	*(handwritten)*
Where can you find this data?	*(handwritten)*
The benchmark for your store	*(handwritten)*

Now, some initial information about the "twin stores". The following number of people entered the two stores during the last given period of time:

	Store A	Store B
Footfall	1,200	900

What do you think may have caused this difference?

_____

_____

_____

_____

What can the store managers do to increase the number of people that come through the door?

_____

_____

_____

_____

Have you written your answers? Before checking them with the answers in the appendix, take a closer look at this indicator on the following pages.

WHICH VARIABLES INFLUENCE THE FOOTFALL?

These are the main variables that influence footfall.

1. The **store's location**: when all other conditions are the same, a store in a location with a lot of traffic whereby it is easy to stop and go in, will be visited by more people (this type of footfall is sometimes referred to as being "caught" because the store has generated this footfall just by being where it is).

2. The **neighbouring competition**: a store without any nearby competitors ("one-of-a-kind") has a relative monopoly and therefore has a higher probability of getting customers through the door. However, we cannot say that the opposite is true, i.e. a store surrounded by many similar stores will not have many customers; there is a concept known as "economies of agglomeration". This relates to areas that contain clusters of many similar stores which increase footfall and thereby benefit them all (for example, the shopping streets in many city centres).

3. The **recognition of the brand** and all the marketing actions implemented by the brand to attract customers: the launch of new products, new collections, contests, advertising, etc.

4. The **reputation of the store** (which will also depend on how many years the store has been open) and all the actions implemented by the store to attract customers: for example, the service rendered to the customers, events organised in the store, local advertising and discount policies agreed with other local operators.

5. The **initial impact from the storefront and window displays** (the quality of the store's exterior, displays in the store windows, the store sign): if customers are "amazed" by what they see from the outside, they are much more likely to enter a store.

6. The **overall quality of the shopping experience**: customers return and speak highly about the store (generating positive word of mouth) if they find quality products at reasonable prices, swift, satisfactory service, and a pleasant environment.

7. **Loyalty programmes**: effective loyalty programmes make it worth for customers to come back and buy from the same store.

WHAT ARE THE STORE MANAGER'S ACTIONABLE LEVERS FOR INCREASING FOOTFALL?

Many of the variables on which footfall depends cannot be directly controlled by the store manager. But this does not mean that you should fail to tackle or passively "put up with" this indicator as if it represented a sort of destiny.

There are many things managers can do to have a positive influence on footfall:

1. **Attend to the entrance** (its design, the store windows, cleaning, an open door, etc.) and avoid "scaring away" customers. For example, customers may be discouraged from entering the store if sales assistants stand too close to the door;

2. **Look after every step of the selling process** so that customers feel motivated to return and speak highly about the store;

3. **Increase the store's attractiveness** by using:

• **Local advertising** (radio, posters and billboards, local newspapers);

• **Agreements with other local operators that are relevant** to the store's target market (transports companies, local hotels, sports clubs, schools and other organisations in the area);

• **Organise your own in-store events**.

4. **Develop long-term relations with the customers** to increase their "loyalty". If a store's sales assistants can build personal relations with some of the customers, that store will then have a group of loyal customers that visit on a regular basis and whereby they can also be invited to special occasions.

2. THE BUYING CUSTOMER: NUMBER OF TRANSACTIONS AND THE CONVERSION RATE

Some people who enter into your store may be converted into customers by making a purchase, which generates a receipt, i.e. a transaction. There are two ways to measure the decision to be converted into customers:

1. ... through the number of transactions:

The number of transactions is the total number of transactions a store does in a given period of time (an hour, day, week, month, or year), irrespective of their amount or of the fact that the same customer may have generated more than one transaction.

What is this indicator called in your business?	

How do I calculate this indicator?

This figure is usually produced automatically by the cash register's software. All transactions must go through the cash register for this figure to be reliable.

Where can you find this data?	

The benchmark for your store	

2. ... and through the conversion rate. This information is only available if the store measures footfall:

The conversion rate is the percentage of people that enter a store and are converted into customers through producing a transaction.

What is this indicator called in your business?	

How do I calculate this indicator?

The conversion rate is the **ratio between the number of people that enter a store** (footfall) and the **number of receipts issued (transactions)**. This is a rough indicator that is subject to systematic errors which are not significant. For example:

- If a customer generates two transactions, the conversion rate "counts" these as if they were done by two different customers;
- If a couple groups their purchases together, the conversion rate will calculate that purchase as if it were made by just one person (hence the couple would have a conversion rate of 50% whereby as if one of the two did not purchase anything).

This is the formula:

$$\frac{Number\ of\ in-store\ visits}{Number\ of\ transactions}$$

Where can you find this data?	

The benchmark for your store	

And now, the results from the twin stores:

	Store A	Store B
Footfall	1,200	900
Number of transactions	360	360
Conversion rate	30%	40%

Imagine that you are a customer. What difference do you think you will find in the two stores?

_____

_____

_____

_____

What could the store manager of Store A do to increase the number of people that buy something in the store?

_____

_____

_____

_____

The two indicators within this chapter measure the same thing, but one contains more information than the other: the conversion rate tells you how many transactions you have done and also tells you how many you have not done!

Given that many stores do not measure footfall, which is essential for calculating the conversion rate, we will look at how to use the two indicators separately.

THE NUMBER OF TRANSACTIONS

What does this indicator measure?

The number of transactions is an indicator that **measures a store's ability to generate purchases**; in other words, it measures **a store's efficacy**. Behind every receipt there is always at least one customer who has come through the door, made a purchase, and paid. The number of transactions is also a metric showing how much work is done in a store as(for example, the number of cars produced by a car manufacturer illustrates the amount of work done in a factory).

Which variables influence the indicator?

Practically each and every one of a store's levers influences the number of transactions, so I'll just mention the variables that have the greatest impact. Let's look at this from the customer's point of view. A customer makes a purchase when he or she:

1. **Finds a product and appreciates its quality**; this means that the choice of products displayed in the store decisively influences the number of transactions;

2. **Finds a conducive sales environment** (if it is a self-service store, the customer should easily locate the product; if it is a full-service store, the customer shouldn't have to wait too long to be served);

3. **Finds exactly what they are looking for** (style, size, and colour: remember how frustrated you feel when the store doesn't have the item you want in your size? Or when you go to the supermarket to buy fresh milk and it is out of stock?);

4. Finds a **price** that meets expectations;

5. Gets the **service** he or she needs (for example, the labels on the shelves are easy to understand, or the sales assistants are readily available and competent);

6. Finds a store with **convenient opening hours** (offering a longer opening hours increases the number of transactions);

7. **Is not bothered by other customers** (i.e. the store is not too crowded: when footfall exceeds a certain limit it reduces the number of transactions because customers "escape" from the store).

Which actionable levers can the store manager use to change the indicator?

Once again the store manager does not normally have all the levers at his or her disposal. These are just some of the main things you can do as a store manager to increase the number of transactions:

1. If you decide the product assortment, the first rule is to **buy** the right quantity of the right things at the right time (obvious but so true!);

2. Be utterly scrupulous about the way you manage the **image of the store** (well-displayed goods, all shelves and displays are full, information is carefully written, prices are clear and understandable, etc.), and create attractive and innovative displays;

3. **Limit the amount of damaged stock**;

4. Align the **prices** with the customers' expectations and with the prices applied by the competition;

5. Carefully manage **peak shopping times**, and organise work in a way that minimises inconvenience for the customers (this is when you are most likely to lose transactions);

6. Raise the sales assistants' level of **product understanding and awareness**;

7. Train sales assistants how to:

• **Welcome and greet the customer**;

• Recognise when the customer needs help and **how to approach him or her**;

• **Handle multiple customers at the same time** during peak shopping times.

THE CONVERSION RATE

What does this indicator measure?

The conversion rate accurately measures the efficacy of a store, so it tells you about the **success of the offering** of the store (products, setting, service, prices): if you compare the number of in-store visits with the number of people that made a purchase, you have a measure of the store's ability to persuade the customers.

You can also see the percentage of customers that were not persuaded by what the store has to offer, or did not find what they were looking for.

Which actionable levers can the store manager use to change the indicator?

The same levers that applied to the number of transactions also apply here: if you want to improve the conversion rate, you need to increase the number of transactions. So I won't repeat the reasons we've already looked at, but I will add a couple of points worth considering.

1. For a sales assistant, the conversion rate indicator is easier to understand than the number of transactions: "converting" a passer-by into a customer is actually a sale assistant's main responsibility. This indicator is very useful when training sales assistants, motivating a store's team, and carrying out assessments.

2. When can I claim to have a "good" conversion rate? Some stores naturally have a very low conversion rate that never gets above 20%: an example of this would be stores with high "fashion" content as their customers visit frequently even when they have no intention of making a purchase. Other stores may achieve up to 50%, such as stores that sell durable goods and/or luxury goods and/or offer high standards of service. In some cases the conversion rate may be even higher, such as grocery stores in which practically every customer that goes into the store tends to buy something.

SALES

And now we finally get to the store's sales (or revenue, as it is also known).

Sales represent the total amount of money paid out by customers using any form of payment to purchase the products or services offered by a store. This figure may be gross, i.e. it includes value added tax (VAT), or net.

How do I calculate sales?

This information is automatically provided by the cash registers. It is the **sum of the amounts of the receipts** issued in a given period of time: the real or virtual money in the drawer of the cash register. Sales are expressed in the currency of the country in which the store is located.

What does this measure?

Sales represent the main measure of the **dimensions of the business**: a commercial enterprise can be defined as "large" or "small" based on the amount of sales that it can generate. So sales measure a store's efficacy and are without doubt the first piece of information to take into consideration when trying to understand how a store is doing.

Sales do not necessarily represent the sole revenue of a commercial organisation as retail can also generate revenue with contributions, from manufacturers and suppliers (this is why the turnover of a commercial enterprise is often higher than its sales). These contributions reward the store for the volume of sales it has generated, or can finance promotional activities.

What is this indicator called in your business?	

Where can you find this data?	

The benchmark for your store	

Let's continue analysing how our twin stores are performing. What these two stores are selling is a mystery to us so the currency they use for their transactions will also remain a mystery. The figures that I've given you are neither in Euros nor in any other known currency. The exercise is about understanding store performance without concentrating on the actual value of the currency, as we are used in our everyday routine at work.

This is the data for the same period:

	Store A	Store B
Footfall	1,200	900
Number of transactions	360	360
Conversion rate	30%	40%
Sales	16,200	15,120

What are your observations?

_____

_____

_____

_____

Which variables influence sales?

Sales are influenced by everything that the store manager does and does not do, and by everything that the people who work in the store (sales assistants, cashiers, warehouse operatives, visual, etc.) actually do and do not do. In a chain store, **sales are also influenced by the decisions made by the people in the head office**. Furthermore, they are greatly **influenced by manufacturers' sales policies**, the macroeconomic situation and by fashion trends.

So sales provide very important data that allows the store manager to understand at a glance how things are progressing.

But aggregate figures do not help those who have to make decisions in the field daily to understand what is really going on. To get a better understanding, which will enable us to take action, we need to split up the data and divide it into more specific components that help us refer to more exact causes.

The overall value of the sales works a bit like a traffic light: if it is green, everything is ok; if it is amber, we need to worry; and if it is red, we've got a serious problem. We need to analyse the situation in more depth in order to understand where we have a problem so that we can intervene.

What are the store manager's actionable levers?

Every actionable lever that he has at his disposal... but you need to read the following chapters!

SALES PER SQUARE METRE

Before we analyse the make-up of the sales figures in more detail, there is a performance indicator that is very useful when we wish to compare stores that are similar but not identical: sales per square metre.

Sales per square metre is the average revenue a store creates for every square metre of selling space. This indicator provides a parameter of the store's efficacy based on the amount of available selling space (two stores are practically never identical).

How do I calculate this indicator?
It is the ratio of sales to the number of square metres available to customers, i.e. selling space (so bear in mind that it does not include the stockroom or any office areas).

This is the formula:

$$\frac{Sales}{Square\ metres\ of\ selling\ space}$$

What does this indicator measure?
Sales per square metre measures **the ability of the available space to generate revenue**, and thereby margins. All other things being equal (location, format, commercial offering, economic situation), it provides a concise assessment about the quality of the business decisions made by the store manager and by the chain.

What is this indicator called in your business?	
Where can you find this data?	
The benchmark for your store	

Let's look at the sales per square metre for the twin stores:

	Store A	Store B
Footfall	1,200	900
Number of transactions	360	360
Conversion rate	30%	40%
Sales	16,200	15,120
Selling space	228 m^2	217 m^2
Sales per m^2	71.05	69.68

What are your observations?

_____

_____

_____

_____

4. BENCHMARKS

Up until now we have focused on the result from one period when analysing the results of the twin stores, which means that we've been looking at a snapshot of only one given moment. The only available information to us was related to the current period, and the only method we had to formulate any hypothesis about the results of the two stores was to make a direct comparison.

In this chapter we'll take a closer look at the importance of making comparisons and explore the three main types of comparison:
- The previous period;
- Other stores' results;
- Budget.

THE IMPORTANCE OF COMPARISONS

Let's start with the first point: why is making comparisons so helpful?

The first answer may seem a bit abstract but it's true: because our brains love to compare things. We can't grasp the extent of a phenomenon unless we have something to measure it by. Imagine you are looking at an imposing, gnarled tree with a child standing next to it. If the tree only comes up to the child's knees, we immediately realise that it is a bonsai; but if the child is barely taller than the tree roots, it's a redwood.

A second, sportier, answer would be: every indicator measures something, and there is a maximum limit to every indicator that is difficult to achieve. For example, every sport has a world record that someone occasionally beats and this represents the best possible result in a given moment. The result has been improved over time by perfecting better training techniques, diet and equipment. By comparing their results with the current record even amateur athletes can set themselves realistic goals and measure their progress.

The third answer relates to the business: the market is more variable than sports results. A result achieved by a store during a period of expansion cannot be replicated during a period of economic crisis. The sales achieved by a store in a high-footfall location, such as a shopping centre for example, cannot be compared with the sales achieved by a store in a quieter area. Price points, inflation, and labour costs are not the same everywhere. This means that always having current, reliable and meaningful parameters is essential when assessing a store's performance.

A FILM TRUMPS A PHOTO: LIKE-FOR-LIKE COMPARISONS

Indicators provide a snapshot that "captures" the situation in a given moment. The snapshot tells you if things are going well or badly, but it doesn't tell you whether they are improving or getting worse.

To get this answer you need more than a photograph; you need a film: you need to compare the results from the current period with those from a previous equivalent period. This is normally called "*like-for-like*" comparison.

For example, you might change your opinion about the twin stores if I told you that these were the footfall and transactions in previous periods:

	Store A		Store B	
	Current period	Previous period	Current period	Previous period
Footfall	1,200	1,250	900	800
Number of transactions	360	387	360	304
Conversion rate	30%	31%	40%	38%

Try playing with this new information.

What is happening in Store A?

_____

_____

_____

_____

And in Store B?

_____

_____

_____

_____

THE IMPORTANCE OF BENCHMARKING

I have already mentioned the importance of having a benchmark and that it is difficult for me to provide "universal" benchmarks in this book that enable you to confirm whether one result is positive and another is negative.

However, benchmarks do exist in reality. Let's see how we can obtain them:

1. If your store is part of a chain, you can compare your results with the company average, or with a group of stores that are similar to yours (*homogeneous cluster*), or even with the *best performer*;

2. If you have an independent store, you can use information provided by trade associations, specialist journals or even talk to people who are in the same line of work. Exchanging information is enriching.

Let's analyse the three main comparison categories.

• Comparing your store with the **company average** tells you if your store is more or less effective than the average of the other stores with regard to a given parameter; this information is rough, very useful and easy to obtain but it doesn't take into account the inhomogeneity of the different stores and the market in which they operate. Therefore we cannot rely on this information.

• Comparing your store with the results produced by a **group of stores** that are **similar** in terms of size, market, and clientele is definitely more effective and specific. If your results are worse than your colleague's, you won't be able to "justify" them as easily by claiming that your situation is different!

• Comparing your store with the **best performer** is challenging. It gives you an exact idea of what can be achieved and therefore it motivates you to think creatively.

I am obviously a fan of benchmarking (namely comparing one's own results with those of other), but before I continue I would like to remind you about something: when you compare the results from two stores, remember that by definition no two stores are absolutely identical and therefore the results from one store are not always transferable to another store, and above all *not in the same way*.

I'll give you an example: a store has really great sales figures and every week the store manager organises a brief meeting before the store opens. During the meeting he discusses the results from the past week, explains any new products that have arrived, and updates the ranking table of the sales assistants based on their individual sales results. At the end of each month he organises an evening when everyone can go out for a meal together. During the evening he awards a prize to the sales assistant that has sold the most over the past month. It's an effective strategy that works well in many stores all over the world. So why don't we all do it?

In theory there is no reason why you can't put into practice something that works well. But let's just imagine for a minute that you are the store manager and these are the conditions in your store:

• You don't have a flair for meetings, you don't like them and you don't believe they work; therefore all your meetings are boring;

• Your store is in the centre of a large city and some of your sales assistants live on the outskirts so they commute in by train; others are mothers with young children; for one reason or another they do not appreciate having to come in early or stay overtime;

• Your store has a rather unfortunate layout that makes it almost impossible for the same sales assistant to follow the customer throughout the entire shopping process; this means each sales assistant is assigned an area and you have incentivised them to "pass the customer" from one to the next; due to this set-up, the individual sales results cannot be used for competitive purposes.

Are you still sure that in order to achieve results that are comparable with the store you have chosen as your benchmark, you need to do the same things as the store manager of that store? I'd say not.

So, in summary:

• Benchmarking with numbers, yes;
• Benchmarking with best practices, to be adapted accordingly.

And now let's get back to our twin stores and see if the introduction of a benchmark has changed the outlook.

| | Store A | Store B | Benchmark | | |
			Company average	Homo-geneous cluster	Best performer
Footfall	1,200	900	980	1,100	1,280
Number of transactions	360	360	285	385	524
Conversion rate	30%	40%	29%	35%	41%

If you were the store manager of Store A, which benchmark would you take more into account?

_____

_____

_____

_____

And if you were the store manager of Store B, which benchmark would you take more into account?

_____

_____

_____

_____

EVEN BUDGETS ARE BENCHMARKS

We have seen how the results from a previous period (*like-for-like*) can provide interesting information. We have discovered that even results from other similar stores (*benchmark*), irrespective of whether they are "allies" or competitors, can help you to understand how your store is doing. Now let's introduce a third benchmark: the *budget*.

The budget is a number that represents a goal for a given period; it is the result of a forecast that takes into account the potential of both the store and the market, as well as possible facts that may have a negative impact, such as a competitor opening a store nearby, a drop in the customer's purchasing power due to a predicted recession, a change in consumers' purchasing patterns, etc. The budget is therefore a well-thought estimated forecast that becomes a goal after a process of deliberation and negotiation.

Not all indicators are worked into the budget: each company selects a few indicators that it believes to be critical to its success, and focuses on those. Sales figures are always one of these indicators.

Now let's look at the results of the twin stores again, and this time I'll put forward two different budgets. You might be amazed to discover that your interpretation of the information will change greatly now that you have this new information.

For example, imagine that this is the budget:

	Store A		Store B	
	Current period	Budget	Current period	Budget
Footfall	1,200		900	
Number of transactions	360	320	360	380
Conversion rate	30%		40%	
Sales	16,200	15,000	15,120	16,000

How can you explain a budget like this?

_____

_____

_____

_____

How does it change your assessment of the results of the two stores?

_____

_____

_____

_____

Or imagine that this is the budget:

	Store A		Store B	
	Current period	Budget	Current period	Budget
Footfall	1,200		900	
Number of transactions	360	400	360	350
Conversion rate	30%		40%	
Sales	16.200	18.000	15,120	14.000

How can you explain a budget like this?

_____

_____

_____

_____

How does it change your assessment of the results of the two stores?

_____

_____

_____

_____

We already knew the average sale per transaction of our two stores: we just had to calculate it. Clearly Store B has the same number of transactions, but they are for a smaller amount on average. Therefore, the customers in that store spend less.

	Store A	Store B
Footfall	1,200	900
Number of transactions	360	360
Conversion rate	30%	40%
Sales	16,200	15,120
Average sale per transaction	45	42

But why do Store B's customers spend less?

Perhaps it has lower prices? Perhaps it sells fewer items but they are more expensive? Perhaps some of the shelves are empty? Perhaps customers cannot find what they are looking for? Perhaps that store's customers visit less often? Perhaps, perhaps, perhaps…

I could go on posing questions. Clearly this information still doesn't give us the whole story. But let's have a closer look.

DEFINITION

The average sale per transaction is the sum that a customer spends on average every time he/she makes a purchase in a store. It is an extremely concise measurement of the store's ability to satisfy customer needs.

How do I calculate this indicator?

It is the ratio of sales to the number of transactions. The average sale per transaction is expressed in the currency of the country where the store is located.

The formula is:

$$\frac{Sales}{No.\,of\,transactions}$$

What is this indicator called in your business?	

Where can you find this data?	

The benchmark for your store	

Which variables influence the indicator?

The average sale per transaction is basically determined by two variables:

1. **How many products does the customer buy on average** in the store (the size of the purchase, measured in average units per transaction);

2. **How much does the customer pay on average for each item** (the "average selling price").

To interpret the average sale per transaction we need to understand its two components:

$$\underset{\text{transaction}}{\text{Average sale per}} = \underset{\text{selling price}}{\text{average}} \quad \times \quad \underset{\text{transaction}}{\text{average units per}}$$

$$\downarrow \qquad\qquad \downarrow \qquad\qquad \downarrow$$

$$\frac{\text{Sales}}{\text{Transactions}} = \frac{\text{Sales}}{\text{Number of units}} \quad \times \quad \frac{\text{Number of units}}{\text{Transactions}}$$

Once you have mastered this magic formula, the business dynamics of your store will no longer be a mystery!

6. UNDERSTANDING THE AVERAGE SALE PER TRANSACTION: AVERAGE SELLING PRICE AND AVERAGE UNITS PER TRANSACTION

This time we are going to start with the twin stores and analyse their transactions:

	Store A	Store B
Footfall	1,200	900
Number of transactions	360	360
Conversion rate	30%	40%
Sales	16,200	15,120
Average sale per transaction	45	42
Average selling price	14	16
No. of units per transaction	3.21	2.63

One possible explanation could be that Store B is more expensive and the customers purchase fewer items per visit.

Is this the only explanation? And anyway, why does this happen?

_____

_____

_____

_____

Let's analyse the indicators individually.

THE AVERAGE SELLING PRICE

The average selling price is the average value of the "lines" in each transaction, i.e. the average amount a customer spends on each chosen product.

A "line" in a transaction may be referred to:
- a single product,
- two or more products packaged & sold together.

Actually some stores, particularly in the food industry, do not just sell their products individually; they sell them in other ways as well:
- Multipacks;
- Bundled offers, in which different yet complementary products are sold together;
- By weight.

In all of these cases the average price of the product does not correspond to the average selling price. Let's look at a couple of examples.

1. The price of a can of tomatoes sold individually may be less than the price of the economy pack containing six cans. But the price of an individual can of tomatoes is definitely less when it is purchased as part of an economy pack. The average selling price registers a higher value when the customer chooses the economy pack, because the customer has purchased a greater quantity but at a lower price.

2. When products are sold by weight (in a delicatessen for example), the average selling price measures the quantity of the product purchased on average by the customers. A low average selling price in the delicatessen department tells us that on average customers purchase low quantities of cold meats per visit.

It is important not to confuse the average selling price with the average price of merchandise offered. For example, let's imagine for the sake of convenience that a store sells just four products at these prices:

Product	Price
Alfa	1
Beta	2
Gamma	3
Delta	4

The average price in this store is 2.5. Let's suppose that the store never runs any promotions, and never offers multipacks. To find out the average selling price in this store we need to know the customers' preferences, i.e. which products do they purchase in larger quantities? If they favour products Alfa and Beta, the average selling price will be lower than 2.5, and if the opposite is true it will be greater than 2.5.

This next table suggests two possible scenarios for how the customers' purchase choices are distributed.

Product	Price	First hypothesis		Second hypothesis	
		No. of pcs sold	Turn-over	No. of pcs sold	Turn-over
Alfa	1	10	10	4	4
Beta	2	20	40	8	16
Gamma	3	8	24	20	60
Delta	4	4	16	10	40
Total		42	90	42	120
Average selling price		2.14		2.85	

As we can see from this example, the average selling price does not measure the average price of the assortment offered by a store (not even when the business formula is based solely on the sale of single products). Instead it measures the average price of the product chosen by the customer. It therefore takes a snapshot of the customer's response to the product assortment offered by the store.

What does this indicator measure?

In stores that choose to mainly or exclusively sell individual products, this indicator measures the price point "preferred" by that store's customers: when product categories and the price line are the same, a store with the lower average selling price will sell larger quantities of economy and/or discounted products. In this case, a low average selling price is synonymous with savings.

In stores that resort extensively to selling multipack products and rely on quantities, the interpretation of this information is more complicated: an increase in the average selling price may actually correspond to increased savings.

How do I calculate this indicator?

It is the ratio of sales to the number of lines per transaction. The average selling price is expressed in the currency of the country where the store is located. This is the formula:

$$\frac{Sales}{No.\,of\,units\,(or\,no.\,of\,lines\,per\,transaction)}$$

What is this indicator called in your business?	
Where can you find this data?	
The benchmark for your store	

Which variables influence the indicator?

The average selling price is mainly influenced by the following factors:

1. The **price** at which, with the same brands, **the products are sold** (convenience);

2. How the **product assortment is structured**: selling cheaper branded products lowers the average selling price (the average level of quality of the assortment);

3. The **type of products that are more often chosen by the customers** (for example, if the customers mainly buy more expen-

sive branded products, the average selling price for that store will be higher);

4. The **percentage of products sold with a discount**; nearly all stores run promotions (discounts, special offers, sales, etc.): each product that is sold at a reduced price lowers the average selling price;

5. The **average pack size**; sometimes products are sold in larger packs to offer customers a way to save money. In this case the average selling price goes up (because a larger pack has a higher price), even if the store offers good value for money (because the unit price is lower);

6. In stores where full-service is a determining factor, the average selling price also measures the **sales assistants' ability to steer the customers** towards purchasing more expensive products (upselling).

Which actionable levers can the store manager use to change the indicator?

As with other indicators, the answer to this question depends on the levers at the store manager's disposal. All of the following actions actually help to change the average selling price:

1. **Raising or lowering the prices** of some products, with the same brands;

2. Selling **cheaper or more expensive products**;

3. Offering **discounts**;

4. **Showcasing** the products that the store wants to push;

5. **Using** merchandising as a lever, i.e. highlighting the products in the displays that the store is pushing to sell;

6. Creating **multipacks**, or selling products individually;

7. Raising the sales assistants' level of **product understanding and awareness**;

8. Training sales assistants to use three specific skills:

   a. **Ask questions** to understand what the customer needs;

   b. **Present the product** using arguments that will convince the customer;

   c. **Overcome any objections to the price.**

AVERAGE UNITS PER TRANSACTION

Average units per transaction measures the average number of items or packs taken to the cash register by customers.

What does this indicator measure?

The store's ability to meet a wide range of the customers' needs (so the size of the purchase). A customer purchases more items in the same store if he/she finds a convincing response to a greater number of needs within that store.

How do I calculate this indicator?

It is the ratio of the total number of units to the number of transactions:

$$\frac{No.\,of\,units}{No.\,of\,transactions}$$

What is this indicator called in your business?	
Where can you find this data?	
The benchmark for your store	

Which variables influence the indicator?

The average units per transaction indicator is primarily influenced by the **size and quality of a store's product assortment**: the *wider and more inclusive* the product assortment, the higher the number of units per transaction.

When the concept and product assortment are the same, the units per transaction indicator is influenced by:

1. **Effective use of merchandising levers** (good space organisation, product presentation, in-store information and directions, and product labelling); customers will actually buy more items if

they are easy to find;

2. **Well-stocked shelves** (which depends on the store's ability to minimise stock-outs); customers don't make a purchase if they cannot find what they want;

3. **Ease of purchase** even in peak shopping times (an overcrowded store reduces the units per transaction because it forces the customer to buy only the bare minimum or essentials);

4. In stores where full-service is a determining factor, the **sales assistants' ability to suggest something extra to the customer** (cross-selling: a complementary and/or additional sale).

Which actionable levers can the store manager use to change the indicator?

The store manager can have a considerable influence on this indicator; irrespective of the business levers he has been delegated. The store manager can:

1. **Manage the display area** to best advantage, checking that it is neat, clean, attractive and appealing; and monitoring that in-store signs are the right place, windows are "perfect" and the customer's path throught the store is easy;

2. **Supervise reordering and restocking shelves and racks** so that the customers' favourite products are always in stock and displayed;

3. **Highlight combinations of complementary products in store displays** (such as, belts near trousers, fruit and jam jars for jam making, curtains and curtain poles);

4. **Manage peak shopping times** to best advantage by ensuring more personnel are on the floor and facilitate the shopping experience and payment process;

5. Train sales assistants how to **suggest**:

• **Complementary items** (one product matches or goes well with another);

• **Alternative items** (this is a particularly important skill as sales assistants can persuade customers to purchase a different product when the one they actually want is not available),

• **Additional items**.

How can I lower prices without making a loss?

How to price a product is a topic worthy of its own book. Explaining all the possible factors that contribute to the definition of a price is not one of my goals in this book, and I have to confess that I don't think I would even be able to do so.

And yet I did say in the previous paragraph that one of the ways to sell more products is to use the price lever, i.e. *lowering prices*. So, if I lower prices, I can increase the number of products that I sell. It's so obvious, but... if I lower my prices, I also earn less. So this choice needs to be done carefully: it is not the kind of decision that one makes lightly.

To decide by how much I can lower a price I need to estimate how many more pieces I will sell and I need to weigh up how this decision will affect the margin generated by that product (I will examine this concept in greater detail in Chapter 9).

Let's look at an example: I currently sell 20 pieces of Product X a week at the unit price of 10. My profit (or margin) on that product is 3. So this is the situation:

Product X

Unit selling price	No. of pcs sold per week	Turnover	Unit margin	Total margin
10	20	200	3	60

The question I ask myself is: what happens to the last column when we change the first? In the following table you will find three different scenarios of increased sales following a price reduction of 10% (from 10 to 9):

Product X: selling price reduced by 10% (9 instead of 10)

Hypothesis	Forecasted no. of pcs sold per week	Total sales	Unit margin	Total margin
1 (limited increase)	25	225	2	50
2 (medium increase)	30	270	2	60
3 (high increase)	35	315	2	70

Hypothesis 3 is clearly very profitable: I have increased both sales and the margin. Hypothesis 2 is also rather interesting: my margin stays the same but I have a significant increase in sales. Hypothesis 1 needs to be evaluated carefully though: sales may have increased slightly but the margin shows a definite loss.

How can I know *beforehand* which of the three hypotheses will happen? I can't: experience can help you to assess the situation but the best way is to formulate a hypothesis, decide and then check the result.

Lowering the price "just a bit" is not enough in some situations. Sometimes the market forces you to sell some products at such low prices that you risk making a loss. The solution should be simple: do not sell a product on which you make a loss. But let's imagine that this specific product is in demand by all customers and sold by all the shops. Customers compare the price displayed in my store with the price in other stores and decide whether or not to enter my store or another store based on this price. This is therefore a "comparable" price that acts as a lure (these prices are often known as "loss leaders" because although the product is sold at below cost price it brings in (leads) customers to the store). So what do we do?

I'd now like to introduce a concept that might help you to decide whether and by how much to lower the price of that individual product: the compensation concept. A store can withstand losses on a single product if it can "spread" the lost margin over all the other products that it sells by increasing their prices.

Let's imagine that we lower the price of Product X until it sells at a loss:

Product X

Unit selling price	No. of pcs sold per week	Total sales	Unit margin	Total margin
6	50	300	-1	-50

The number of pieces sold obviously rises but this is not good news for my margin: the more I sell, the worse it gets! At the very least I need to recoup the 50 that I am losing by increasing the margin on the other products in the store.

Let's imagine that in addition to Product X my store sells another 1,000 products per week at an average price of 5.21: by increasing the selling price of each of these products by 0.05 (thereby taking the average price to 5.26) I will have recouped my negative margin on Product X.

However, if I wish to also recoup the margin that I lost compared to when I sold Product X at 10 (i.e. the margin of 60 that the product gave me before I lowered the price), I will need to recoup even more. In this case I will need to increase the average price by 0.11 so that it goes up to 5.32. Will my customers accept this new price point?

Obviously the operation is not as simple as I have described it. Increasing the price of all products in the same way is not advisable; for a start not all the products have the same price. Furthermore, more than one product needs to be compensated so the price increase generated by the compensation is higher than the one described in my example. But this is the basic concept nonetheless.

THE CONCEPT OF PRODUCT CLASSIFICATION

Products are usually classified into product categories (or families). All the products that fulfil the same customer need are grouped together in the same category, e.g. having something to wear, eating, home decor, travel communications, etc.

As with any other classification system, the categories may then be divided into sub-categories, into sub-sub-categories and so on until you get down to single product on sale in a store.

As an example, let's look at the need to have something to wear, known as "apparel". From a business perspective talking about apparel is too generic. So we need to be more specific and create a product classification tree like this:

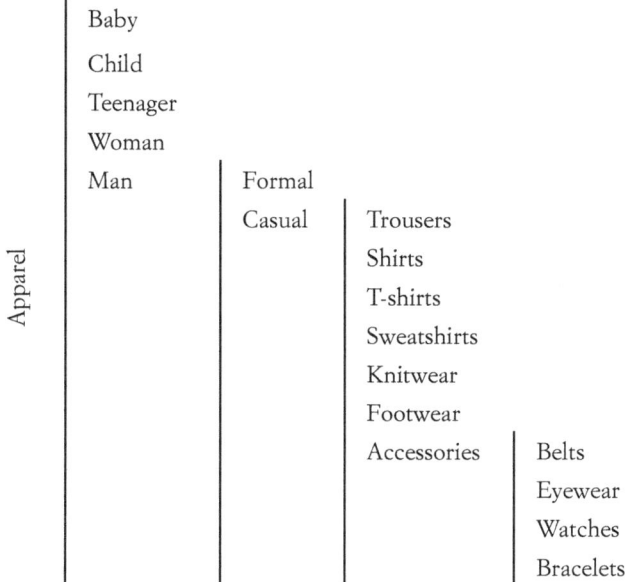

Apparel				
Baby				
Child				
Teenager				
Woman				
Man	Formal			
	Casual	Trousers		
		Shirts		
		T-shirts		
		Sweatshirts		
		Knitwear		
		Footwear		
		Accessories	Belts	
			Eyewear	
			Watches	
			Bracelets	

I didn't want to bore you so I haven't explored every branch in detail but I think it adequately illustrates the idea. Every store sells products that belong to multiple categories or sub-categories. To get a better understanding of the sales results and to understand exactly what the customer buys and does not buy, sales need to be divided into categories.

SALES PER CATEGORY

The overall sales results (turnover, number of units and/or number of pieces sold, average selling price, average price) can be broken down into categories. This provides a more detailed picture of what the store is actually selling.

What does this indicator measure?

Sales per category measures how the different categories contribute to (or impact) the store's results, in terms of both sales revenue (generated sales) and volume (the number of pieces sold and units generated through cash registers).

How do I calculate this indicator?

The following is calculated for each category:

• The sales revenue generated (absolute value and % of the total sales);

• The volume generated (absolute value and % of the total number of pieces sold).

This information is normally generated by the cash register's software.

What is this indicator called in your business?	
Where can you find this data?	
The benchmark for your store	

Which variables influence the sales per category?

Whether a category carries greater or lesser importance is influenced by different factors. I'll just mention some of the key factors. A category "sells well" if:

1. The **quality of the products** on display matches the customer's expectations;

2. The **products are displayed well**, i.e. tidy, clean, with all the information that enables a customer to choose the product;

3. The **products are on the shelves or racks**;

4. The **prices are good value for money**;

5. **The store has no other very strong competitors nearby** (in terms of extensive product range and/or price) for that particular category;

6. **The sales assistants are knowledgeable about the category**, appreciate it and know how to sell it.

7. Enough **space has been dedicated to the category** so that situations of overcrowding (practically) never occur that may prejudice the sale;

8. It is **featured in store windows and/or in-store display areas**;

9. It is often **featured in special offers** run by the store.

What are the store manager's actionable levers for improving a category's results?

Most of the variables listed here are ones that can be influenced by the store manager. In addition to selecting different products and reviewing the price point, the primary actions that the store manager can take to increase a category's sales are:

1. Ensure that the **products are always in stock**;

2. Improve **product presentation** by always keeping the selling space for that category neat and tidy;

3. Raise the sales assistants' level of **product understanding and awareness** and improve their ability to sell to the customer;

4. **Draw attention to the products** and check that all

written information is legible and correct;

5. Place some of the category's products in **strategic positions** (in the store window, at the entrance, in promotional areas within the store, near the cash registers);

6. Train sales assistants **how to suggest** complementary and additional items;

7. Organise **promotions** for that category's products.

Let's go back to our twin stores and see how their sales are structured. To keep things simple I've decided that these stores only handle three categories.

These are their figures:

categories	Store A					Store B				
	Sales	% sales	No. of pcs	% pcs	Average price	Sales	% sales	No. of pcs	% pcs	Average price
1	9,720	60%	747	65%	13.00	7,560	50%	521	55%	14.50
2	4,860	30%	316	27%	15.40	3,024	20%	172	18%	17.60
3	1,620	10%	94	8%	17.20	4,536	30%	252	27%	18.00
Total	16,200	100%	1,157	100%	14.00	15,120	100%	945	100%	16.00

What do you think were the strategies followed by Store A?

_____

_____

_____

_____

What advice would you give to the store manager of Store A to improve the results?

_____

_____

_____

_____

What do you think were the strategies followed by Store B?

_____

_____

_____

_____

What advice would you give to the store manager of Store B to improve the results?

_____

_____

_____

_____

8. CROSS-SELLING INDICATORS: NUMBER OF CATEGORIES PER TRANSACTION AND PENETRATION

Cross-selling is when a store sells products from different product categories to the same customer. By way of example, let's compare these two transactions, or receipts, from a greengrocer's shop:

Receipt 1	Receipt 2
Chestnuts	Pears
Apples	Chestnuts
Oranges	Spinach
Pears	Red wine

Both the transactions contain the same number of items, and they might even come to the same amount, but there is a big difference between the two: the customer with receipt 2 found that the store met more or his/ her needs and made a more varied purchase.

THE NUMBER OF CATEGORIES PER TRANSACTION

Let's look at a new indicator: the **number of categories per transaction.** When we use this indicator to assess the two transactions we can see that they are very different.

	Receipt 1	Receipt 2
No. of units per transaction	4	4
No. of categories per transaction	1	3

In the first case the four items purchased by the customer belong to the same category (fruit), while the second transaction involved three different three categories diverse (fruit, vegetables and wine).

The number of categories per transaction is the number of categories purchased on average by customers during one visit.

What does this indicator measure?

It measures the range of the customer's purchase, i.e. how many of the customer's different needs does the store meet during one visit.

This indicator is particularly well suited to small stores in which full-service has a significant impact on results. It actually enables us to take a snapshot of cross-selling from the customer's point of view, measuring the seller's ability to explore the customer's needs and offer suitable products.

How do I calculate this indicator?

Count the number of product categories in each transaction; if it contains multiple products from the same category, we only count that category once. We then work out the average number of categories per transaction.

This is usually calculated automatically by the cash register's software. This is the formula:

$$\frac{No.\ of\ categories\ in\ trans.\ 1 + no.\ of\ cat.in\ trans.\ 2 + no.\ of\ cat.\ in\ trans.\ n}{Total\ no.\ of\ transactions}$$

What is this indicator called in your business?	

Where can you find this data?	

The benchmark for your store	

Which variables influence the data?

The number of categories per transaction is mainly influenced by four variables:

1. The store's **choices of product assortment**;
2. The store's **promotional choices**;
3. **Displays** that make the products easy to find and encourage impulse buying;
4. The sales assistants' ability to **suggest product combinations**.

Which actionable levers can the store manager use to change the indicator?

The first variable (product assortment) is a prerequisite (you cannot sell what you don't have!), but often does not fall within the store manager's control. As a general rule, **broadening the product assortment** offered by a store produces good results if the new categories complement the other products and if they are given enough display space.

The other three variables are the ones that make a difference to day-to-day management. The number of categories per transaction can be increased by devising promotions **that incentivise the simultaneous purchase of multiple categories**, or by offering "packages" of related products that are good value for money.

If the store manager wants to work on *how the goods are displayed*, he/she can focus on:

- **Display combinations**, by placing products that are used simultaneously next to each other, e.g. in store windows, in-store display areas, and on the shelves or racks, even if they belong to different product categories;

- **Impulse buys**, by drawing attention to products that customers do not expect to find or that are not the main reason why they have entered a certain store.

In terms of the staff's *sales techniques*, the store manager can train or teach sales assistants:

- **Product understanding and awareness**;

• How to **ask questions to understand what the customer needs** and how they use the product;

• How to use a more personal approach when **presenting the product**;

• How to **suggest** complementary and additional items.

PENETRATION

Another way of taking a snapshot of a store's cross-selling ability is to measure the **penetration** of the different categories (or "**uptake**").

Category penetration is the percentage of transactions that contain at least one item from that category.

Let's use the example of the two transactions we saw at the beginning of this chapter, and imagine that the store only produced these two receipts. Based on these figures we can say that the penetration of the three categories sold by the store is as follows:

• Fruit:	100%
• Wine:	50%
• Vegetables:	50%

What does this indicator measure?

Penetration measures the ability of a product category to "win over" a store's customers. It doesn't actually measure the volume of the purchase (as we saw previously, we get this information from the incidence), but the number of customers that choose at least one item from that category (the "percentage of persuaded customers").

Low penetration tells us that not many of the total number of customers that come into the store buy products from that category: the store is not "strong" in that category, or at any rate is not recognised as such, or the category is not displayed in a way that attracts and persuades customers. High penetration tells us the opposite; many customers come to the store specifically to buy products from that category and the category is one of that store's strengths (and attractions), or that once many customers are through the door they are attracted and persuaded by the store offering.

So penetration measures cross-selling from the trader's point of view because it provides an answer to this question: how many of the customers that walk by my products are attracted enough to buy them?

This indicator is particularly suited to large stores in which different categories are distributed throughout the space and where a considerable number of purchasing decisions are made without the help of sales assistants.

How do I calculate this indicator?

Choose a category and count the number of transactions that contained at least one item from that category; if a transaction has multiple products from the same category, we only count that category once. This number is compared with the total number of transactions.

This is usually calculated automatically by the cash register's software. This is the formula:

$$\frac{No.\ of\ transactions\ with\ that\ category}{Total\ no.\ of\ transactions} \times 100$$

What is this indicator called in your business?	
Where can you find this data?	
The benchmark for your store	

Which variables influence the indicator?

Category penetration is influenced by the same variables that we analysed for the number of categories per transaction:

1. The variety of **the product assortment** and the dedicated spaces;

2. The store's **promotional choices**;

3. **Displays** that make the products easy to find and encourage impulse buying;

4. The sales assistants' ability to **suggest product combinations**.

Which actionable levers can the store manager use to change the indicator?

To increase a category's penetration, the store manager can implement all the actions described for the number of categories per transaction as well as those described in Chapter 6.

Now let's try a rather demanding exercise in analysis: study the receipts produced during a given day by our two stores one by one, and calculate these two new indicators.

Turn the page!

These are receipts produced by **Store A** on a "normal" day.

Receipt no.	No. of category 1 products	No. of category 2 products	No. of category 3 products	No. of units	No. of categories
1	1			1	1
2	1			1	1
3		1		1	1
4		2		2	1
5	2			2	1
6	1	1		2	2
7		1	1	2	2
8			2	2	1
9	2			2	1
10	2			2	1
11	2			2	1
12	2			2	1
13	2			2	1
14		2	1	3	2
15	3			3	1
16	1	2		3	2
17	2	1		3	2
18	1	2		3	2
19	3			3	1
20	3			3	1
21	1	1	1	3	3
22	3			3	1
23	3			3	1
24	3	1		4	2
25		2	2	4	2
26	2		2	4	2

Receipt no.	No. of category 1 products	No. of category 2 products	No. of category 3 products	No. of units	No. of categories
27	3	1		4	2
28	2	2		4	2
29	2	2		4	2
30	4			4	1
31	3	1	1	5	3
32	4	1		5	2
33	3	2		5	2
34	5			5	1
35	6			6	1
36	3	3		6	2
Total	**75**	**28**	**10**	**113**	**55**

For this sample of transactions calculate:

- the average units per transaction _____
- the average number of categories per transaction _____
- category 1 penetration _____
- category 2 penetration _____
- category 3 penetration _____

These are receipts produced by **Store B** on a "normal" day.

Receipt no.	No. of category 1 products	No. of category 2 products	No. of category 3 products	No. of units	No. of categories
1	1			1	1
2	1			1	1
3	1			1	1
4			1	1	1
5			1	1	1
6	1		1	2	2
7	1	1		2	2
8	1	1		2	2
9	1	1		2	2
10	1	1		2	2
11	1		1	2	2
12	1		1	2	2
13	1		1	2	2
14	1	1		2	2
15		1	1	2	2
16		1	1	2	2
17	1		1	2	2
18			2	2	1
19	1	1	1	3	3
20	1	1	1	3	3
21	2	1		3	2
22	2	1		3	2
23	2	1		3	2
24	3			3	1
25	3			3	1
26	3			3	1

Receipt no.	No. of category 1 products	No. of category 2 products	No. of category 3 products	No. of units	No. of categories
27	3			3	1
28	3			3	1
29	2	1	1	4	3
30	1	1	2	4	3
31	2	1	1	4	3
32	1	1	2	4	3
33	3		1	4	2
34	3		1	4	2
35	3		1	4	2
36	2	1	2	5	3
Total	53	17	24	94	68

For this sample of transactions calculate:
- the average units per transaction _____
- the average number of categories per transaction _____
- category 1 penetration _____
- category 2 penetration _____
- category 3 penetration _____

Finished? Or did you get stuck on the calculations?

Well, these are the results of the two stores, and I've compared them with the results from chain's best performer:

	Store A	Store B	Best performer
No. of units per transaction	3.14	2.61	3.44
No. of categories per transaction	1.53	1.89	1.96
Penetration			
- Category 1	83.33%	86.11%	86.82%
- Category 2	50.00%	47.22%	50.98%
- Category 3	19.44%	55.56%	58.03%

What's your analysis?

_____

_____

_____

Now try putting together all the information you have about the twin stores and identify some areas that could be improved upon for Store A:

_____

_____

_____

... and for Store B:

_____

_____

_____

Now it's time to talk about margins, i.e. the difference between **a business's revenue and the total costs incurred to produce it**.

There are various "intermediate" margins that measure the result by subtracting just some of the costs incurred. In this chapter I will show you two ways to calculate the margin which are particularly helpful when managing a retail.

THE FIRST MARGIN

The first margin (or "gross margin", or "cash margin") is the difference between the selling price and the cost of the sold items (the price paid by the retailer to the supplier). For the sake of convenience, it is normally calculated net of VAT. The margin can be applied to overall sales figures, different categories or subcategories, individual products, and individual suppliers.

What does this indicator measure?

The average profitability of the sales in a given period of time. This first margin also contains any discounts (please see the next chapter) and provides a snapshot of the overall result of a store or specific category.

How do I calculate this indicator?

Net sales (i.e. sales without VAT) less the cost of goods sold without VAT. Suppliers sometimes provide goods free of charge: to work out the cost of goods sold we therefore need to include the value of the free goods in the calculation, thereby lowering the average cost price. This is the formula:

- $Value = \dfrac{Total\ sales - cost\ of\ goods\ sold}{Total\ sales} \times 100$
- $Percentage = \dfrac{Total\ sales - cost\ of\ goods\ sold}{Total\ sales} \times 100$

What is this indicator called in your business?	

Where can you find this data?	

The benchmark for your store	

Which variables influence the indicator?

The first margin percentage is influenced by:

- **Cost price** (including any free products and extra discounts offered by the supplier for promotions);
- **Selling price**;
- **Discounts implemented by the store**.

In addition the parameters I've listed, the absolute first margin also depends on the quantity of products sold. This is why it is interesting to consider the **margin mix** (explained in the next pages), which represents the overall result of sales activities, rather than just the percentage of margin generated by individual items.

What are the store manager's actionable levers?

In terms of the cost price, **negotiating with the supplier** is the main lever that enables you to improve this indicator.

In terms of the sales, there are other things that can be done:

1. Decide the "best possible" **selling price**, avoiding prices that are too high (and scare off the customer), but also avoiding unnecessarily low prices (which penalise the store);

2. Manage **orders** to best advantage so that you are not forced to offer discounts later on to get rid of excessive amounts of stock;

3. Take a targeted approach to using **discounts**, compensating whenever possible;

4. **Improve the** "sales mix", i.e. the composition of purchases made on average by customers by developing cross-selling tech-

niques and steering the customer towards products with higher sales margins.

This is the first margin for the twin stores:

	Store A	Store B	Company average
First margin (%)	38.50%	41.00%	37.50%
First margin (value)	6,237	6,199	

How do you explain Store A's results?

_____

_____

_____

_____

How do you explain Store B's results?

_____

_____

_____

_____

THE SECOND MARGIN

The second margin (or "trading margin") is derived from acquisitions and from the relationship with the supplier and is therefore connected to the product. This second margin takes into account the so-called "**manufacturer promotions to trade**", which are contributions in money offered by manufacturers and suppliers to the distributor in certain situations, for example, when the store buys a larger volume of products, or runs a promotion featuring some of the supplier's products.

As the supplier has offered the distributor these sums, they must be added to the sales, as in this example:

Sales	+	1,000	100%
Cost of goods sold	-	700	70%
First margin	+	**300**	**30%**
Manufacturer promotions	+	50	5%
Second margin (trading margin)	+	**350**	**35%**

We are not going to explore this second margin in this handbook as it would require a very lengthy chapter and distance us from our goal.

THE MARGIN MIX

To understand how we get to a margin, it's essential to understand the concept of the margin "mix". Let's look at an example. You sell only three products in your store with this margin:

	First margin
Product A	10%
Product B	15%
Product C	20%

What is the average margin with which your store operates?

_____

If your answer was "15" (i.e. the mean of 10, 15 and 20), you're wrong; if your response was "I don't know", you answered correctly. To work out this figure we need to take into account the number of pieces sold and the selling price.

Let's try again:

	First margin	Selling price	Number of pcs sold	Total sales	Total margin
Product A	10.00%	200	100	20,000	2,000
Product B	15.00%	150	250	37,500	5,625
Product C	20.00%	100	500	50,000	10,000
Total	**16.40%**		850	107,500	17,625

Your store is operating with a margin mix of 16.4°%, and an average selling price of 126. This is due to the fact that the cheapest product is also the one with the highest margin and largest sales.

What happens when the number of pieces sold for Product A increases and the number of pieces sold for Product C goes down?

To keep things simple I'll just invert the two numbers:

	First margin	Selling price	Number of pcs sold	Total sales	Total margin
Product A	10.00%	200	500	100,000	10,000
Product B	15.00%	150	250	37,500	5,625
Product C	20.00%	100	100	10,000	2,000
Total	**11.95%**		850	147,500	17,625

The result is quite interesting: sales rise from 107,500 to 147,500 (+ 37%) because Product A costs more; the average selling price rises to 174; the absolute margin stays the same while the percentage margin drops by almost 5 %! So we can say that the margin mix in this store has gone down as it needs to sell a larger quantity of products to achieve the same result in terms of value.

So in summary, the overall margin result of a store depends on the margin mix, which is the result of the combined effect of multiple factors:

- The margin of the individual products sold;
- The selling price at which each product is sold;
- The number of pieces sold for each product.

Understanding how the margin reacts to an increase or reduction in each one of these three factors is not instinctive; sometimes a decision may produce the opposite effects to the ones you expected. This is why before you make a decision it is always a good idea to run a *simulation* of its effects.

For example, let's imagine that the price of a product has been increased and the customer has reacted by buying fewer pieces. An increase in the unit margin percentage could lead to an overall decrease in total margin.

This case could be illustrated by these figures:

Product "Alfa"	Before	After	Difference	Difference %
Selling price	10	11	+1	+10%
Unit margin (value)	2	3	+1	+50%
Unit margin (%)	20%	27.3%	+7.3	+36.3%
Pcs sold	100	40	-60	-60%
Total margin (value)	**200**	**120**	**-80**	**-40%**

This phenomenon can get even more complicated: the customer often reacts to a product's price increase by buying similar products. Let's imagine that a considerable share of the sales moves to another product, whose price has not been altered, with which the store has lower margins though.

Product "Beta"	Before	After	Difference	Difference %
Selling price	9	9	-	-
Unit margin (value)	1	1	-	-
Unit margin (%)	11.1%	11.1%	-	-
Pcs sold	50	110	+60	+120%
Product margin (value)	**50**	**110**	**+60**	**+120%**

If we calculate the margin mix, we realise that the operation has not been particularly profitable:

	Before	After	Difference	Difference %
Alfa + Beta total sales (value)	1,450	1,430	-20	-1,4%
Alfa + Beta margin mix (value)	250	230	-20	-8%
Alfa + Beta margin mix (%)	17.2%	16.1%	-1.2	-6.7%

So in summary, I thought I'd make a profit but I lost out on sales and my margins as well!

The promotion is a way to increase the number of transactions and the average sale per transaction but has a detrimental effect on the average price of products sold. The main instrument is the **discount**, i.e. a temporary reduction of the selling price.

DIFFERENT TYPES OF DISCOUNT

There are several ways a store can offer discounts:

- **Unconditional discounts** on selected products (such as or price cuts);
- When a customer **buys an increased number of identical products** (for example, the classic "3x2"), or buys a larger quantity of a product (larger packages);
- Discounts on predetermined **product combinations** (such as the joint purchase of a television and a DVD player, for example);
- Discounts based on the **overall volume of the purchase**, irrespective of the types of products bought (for example, spend at least XX and get YY% off your entire purchase);
- **Delayed discounts** (if you spend at least XX today, I guarantee a discount tomorrow with a voucher or coupon).

I'm not going to go into meticulous detail about the various dynamics, advantages and disadvantages of the different promotional options, nor do I plan to examine the question of who pays for the promotions (the supplier or the distributor). I'm just focusing on KPIs: how can we take a snapshot of the impact promotions have on a store's results?

THE OBJECTIVES OF PROMOTIONS

The main results one can expect to see from a promotion are:

1. **Increased footfall**, which measures a promotion's ability to attract customers to the store who would not have otherwise crossed the threshold;

2. An increase in the **number of pieces sold** for products or categories featured in the promotions;

3. A drop in the **margin** percentage and an increase (or no change) in the margin in terms of **absolute value**, once again for products or categories featured in the promotions;

4. **Increased sales** of products and categories that are not featured in the promotions as a result of the promotion's ability to attract customers to the store (the "Seeing as I'm here, I'll buy this too" effect), which is measured as an increase in overall sales and the total margin in absolute value.

When we want to have an idea of how successful a promotion is, we need to duly measure each of these four indicators in turn, and compare the results from the previous period (or from an equivalent period with no promotions) with the results from the promotional period. Assessing the effectiveness of a promotion is often known as debriefing.

PROMOTIONS: LAUDABLE OR SHAMEFUL?

Before we analyse the KPIs relating to promotions, I'd like to ask you to ponder this provocative question: are promotions the result of a purchasing error, a necessary evil, or an effective marketing lever, an opportunity to offer customers a "good deal" and thereby lure them into our stores with the ultimate goal of improving turnover and margins?

Both "positions" have their supporters in the big world of commerce, and there are naturally an infinite number of shades of grey in between. The decision about which position to take is a strategic one. Retail chains in the fashion and luxury segments of the market are often renowned for their desire to limit the impact of promotional policies (or even omit them all together); however, multibrand retailers in both the food and non-food industries see the promotional policy as an opportunity to increase footfall, sales and market share, strengthen customer loyalty, and improve margins.

PERCENTAGE OF REVENUE FROM PROMOTIONS

In addition to duly evaluating each and every promotion, we can concisely measure the impact of promotions by using an indicator known as the percentage of income from promotions.

The percentage of income from promotions is the percentage of sales revenue produced by using any form of direct or delayed discount. It can be calculated on the turnover as a whole, or on sales in different categories.

What does this indicator measure?

The results of efforts made by a store to attract customers or to increase their propensity to purchase from that store. The percentage of revenue from promotions measures the commercial function of the categories handled by a store: categories with a high percentage of revenue from promotions are designed to attract customers, generate footfall and increase the units per transaction, while categories with a low percentage of revenue from promotions serve to generate margins and increase customer loyalty. A high percentage of revenue from promotions knocks down the margin, unless suppliers have contributed to the promotion with extra discounts, or provided funding or free goods. But this indicator does not provide an exact measurement of the magnitude of the promotional efforts as sales obtained with different discounts are represented in the same way.

How do I calculate this indicator?

Once you have the sales results from a given period, you can calculate the percentage of revenue from promotions by adding all sales with a discount and then compare them to the total sales (products sold at full price and at a discounted price). This is the formula:

$$\frac{Total\ sales\ with\ discounted\ price}{Total\ sales} \times 100$$

What is this indicator called in your business?	

Where can you find this data?	

The benchmark for your store	

Which variables influence the indicator?

In order for a promotion to be successful, i.e. the customer actually made a purchase, it must be of interest to the customer and well-advertised. The percentage of income from promotions is basically determined by two factors:

1. A store's **promotional choices** (which products, with which discount, when);

2. The store's ability to **communicate the promotion to the customer** outside the store with leaflets, advertising, etc. and also inside the store through merchandising.

How can I interpret the information?

If the percentage of revenue from promotions is high, it's a good sign. But are things going badly if it's low? Or is the opposite true?

Interpreting data from promotions isn't easy and, as I mentioned earlier, it depends the sale strategy you chose. On the one hand, we have the dream of every trader: to sell all products at full price. On the other hand, we have proof that promotions:

• Attract new customers or bring back customers who are forsaking the store;

• Increase the quantities of products sold;

• Motivate customers to try new products;

• Help to clear products at risk of becoming obsolete.

Another factor worth consideration is that if all businesses are running promotions, avoidance is not an option (or is very difficult to do). As a general rule, I would say that promotions are "healthy" if they help to increase sales and margins. If a store increases the percentage of revenue from promotions, but sales continue to drop, then it definitely has a problem: the percentage of revenue from promotions and sales *must* be directly proportional.

What are the store manager's actionable levers?

If the store manager is in charge of how the promotion is structured, he/she can decide the **key promotional choices**:
- Which products to offer;
- At what price;
- For how long;
- How to present them.

When formulating a promotion it is helpful to run some simulations, which enable you to estimate the result you can expect given certain circumstances.

If the store manager is not the one to decide the promotion, his/her main responsibility will be to manage it, i.e.:

1. **Order the correct quantity of products**;
2. **Display them** effectively;
3. Ensure that sales assistants properly **support the promotion**;
4. Monitor the results during the promotion so that **action can be promptly taken** if the products do not sell (or if they sell more quickly than anticipated).

Let's visit our twin stores again to check their promotional policies. This is the data relating to the percentage of income from promotions in the two stores:

	Store A	Store B	Company average
Category 1	21%	17%	22%
Category 2	18%	14%	17.6%
Category 3	5%	7%	8%
Total	18.50%	13.40%	18.07%

How would you interpret these results?

_____

_____

_____

_____

What suggestions could you offer the two store managers?

_____

_____

_____

_____

MARKDOWNS

A second indicator that allows us to measure how promotions are going is the markdown (percentage or absolute value).

The markdown is a reduction in the price of a product. Once the "full" selling price of a product has been decided, any reduction in that price is a markdown, and consequently results in a net loss in margins. Measuring the total markdowns provides an exact idea of the advantage given to the customer.

What does this indicator measure?

The overall amount of discounts carried out in a given period and/or in certain category, i.e. the **value of the margin invested** by the store (the revenue sacrificed by the retailer in anticipation of a higher volume of sales).

Two conditions determine whether the indicator has any significance:

1. The selling price of the products must be relatively stable over time, or the markdown must be offered only for a very short period of time (for example, end-of-day discounts on fruit and vegetables at a wholesale market);

2. The store must not compensate for markdowns (if the price reduction imposed on one product is compensated for by a price increase on another product, the markdown percentage ceases to provide reliable data).

The markdown indicator is used above all to measure the efficacy of sales, i.e. discounts offered with the aim of clearing stock that would otherwise become obsolete and unsellable (this applies to seasonal goods, which are mainly sold in a certain period of the year, or to products that are nearing their natural "expiry date").

How do I calculate this indicator?

To calculate how much a store has invested in markdowns, we need to add up all the discounts. This generates a (theoretical) value that simultaneously represents the overall savings made by customers in a given period and the margin reduction borne by the store.

The markdown percentage shows the ratio of this value to the total sales. This is the formula:

$$Value = total\ markdowns$$

$$Percentage = \frac{Value\ of\ markdowns}{Total\ sales} \times 100$$

What is this indicator called in your business?	
Where can you find this data?	
The benchmark for your store	

Which variables influence the indicator?

I would like to add an observation to what I said earlier about the percentage of revenue from promotions. The quantity of mark-downs that a store has to resort to in order to clear stock depends mainly on three factors:

1. The **quality of the purchased products** (the right products at the right time and in the right quantities);

2. Chance factors, such as **seasonal occurrences** (for example, a very cold winter will motivate customers to purchase more warm clothes);

3. The **sales assistants' sales skills** (i.e. their ability to sell products at full price).

What are the store manager's actionable levers for reducing markdowns?

The observations about the percentage of revenue from promotions also apply in this context. To minimise the need to resort to markdowns, you need to:

1. **Order the correct quantity of products**;

2. **Display them** effectively;

3. Ensure that the sales assistants **provide customers with all the help they need** when making a purchase.

Let's go back to our twin stores before we finish the chapter. This is the markdown data at the end of a sales period:

	Store A	Store B	Company average
Value	1,200	730	
Percentage	7.41%	4.83%	5.50%

How would you interpret these results?

_____

_____

_____

_____

What suggestions could you offer the two store managers?

_____

_____

_____

_____

Imagine a store that has generated 1,000 transactions in a month. How many customers bought something in that store?

————————————

If you said, "a thousand", it's time to have a good think about the difference between customers and transactions.

I'll give you an example. Imagine that 120 families (about 400 inhabitants) live in a village. Now in this village there is a baker who sells a few essential foodstuffs in addition to the bread and other baked goods that he makes. Many of the people that live in this village shop in his store. Tourists and visiting relatives often pass through the village as well.

How many customers does our baker have?

In reality the baker knows practically all of his customers personally, but he has never bothered to count them. So he decides to do his own little bit of market research: he gets a notebook and every day he jots down who comes in, who buys and how much they spend.

And here are his results. The baker had a total of 186 customers, grouped here according to their buying habits:

- 16 customers bought something practically every day;
- 30 customers bought something every 2-3 days;
- 40 customers came in once a week;
- 100 customers came in only once during the month.

The baker recorded his results in a table:

No. of transactions by the same person during the month	No. of customers	Average no. of transactions per head	% customers	Total transactions	% transactions
20 to 30	16	25	8.6%	400	40%
8 to 19	30	10	16.1%	300	30%
2 to 7	40	5	21.5%	200	20%
1	100	1	53.8%	100	10%
All customers	186	5.4	100%	1,000	100%

The baker understands one important thing from this analysis: the vast majority of his business depends on a rather limited number of people – **the "loyal" customers**.

But how much of his turnover is reliant on loyal customers? The baker decides to name each of the four customer categories and calculates the average sale per transaction and the total amount that every single customer has spent in his store during the month for each category. These are the results of his analysis:

Frequency	No. of customers	No. of transactions	Average no. of transactions per head	Average sale per transaction	Average monthly spend	Total sales	% sales
Daily	16	400	25	10	250	4,000	24.5%
Every other day	30	300	10	25	250	7,500	46%
Weekly	40	200	5	18	90	3,600	22%
Monthly	100	100	1	12	12	1,200	7.5%
All customers	186	1,000	5.4	16.3	87.6	16,300	100%

And this leads him make to another very interesting discovery: 25% of his customers account for 70% of his sales. He also discovers that customers that visit daily buy fewer items per visit. This helps him to realise that the first two categories of customers, those who come daily and every other day, are practically as "loyal" as each other because the overall amount that they spend is practically identical.

So he basically discovers that the **loyal customers are the most profitable**.

Let's leave our example now and see what the definition of loyalty is in the language of KPIs. Here it is:

Loyalty = Frequency x Average purchase

In a given period,

the total amount spent by a customer in a store	is =	the number of visits by the customer	multiplied by	that customer's average sale per transaction

Loyal customers spend a significant part of their "budget" in a store; they visit it frequently and on average spend "a lot". I mentioned the word budget because every family distributes its income between the various expenses that need to be paid during a certain period: expenses for the house, grocery bills, money for clothing, unexpected expenses, etc. In terms of statistics, we can say that **every family has a monthly budget for each product category**. The size of this budget naturally depends on how many people are in the family, purchasing power (or wealth) and lifestyle: however the budget for each category always statistically remains within given limits.

For example, our baker knows that some people eat more bread and others eat less: but he also knows that you can't spend more than a certain amount on bread. The existence of a "family category budget" explains why increasing the store's number of categories is practically an inescapable choice if the store wishes to increase its turnover.

Ok, so now we have understood that loyalty is important, let's ask ourselves how we can improve it.

At first glance it's simple: we need to satisfy the customers. And to do this we need to **know who they are so we can "recognise" them** when they come into the store. We need to know their names, learn their preferences, know what their occupations are, and how their families are made up.

This is why we have loyalty programmes: if I can track my customers' purchases, I will then be able to identify their preferences and buying habits. With this invaluable information I can make more effective business choices. If I know who you are and what you buy, I can actually:

- Ensure you find your favourite products (and thereby remove the ones that you don't like from the product assortment);
- Offer you discounts on your favourite products;
- Better predict your purchases and be more precise when ordering;
- Invite you to the store when I have products that will interest you.

Basically, if I want **to increase a customer's loyalty, I need to** be more effective than my competitors when it comes to **satisfying the customer's needs and offering "cumulative" advantages**, i.e. advantages that increase as the amount spent by the customer in my store increases.

When described like this, loyalty is good for stores where the customer is a frequent visitor. The logic applied to the baker's transactions can also work for all grocery stores and if the right adjustments are made, it can also be applied to non-food stores that offer relatively high purchase frequency categories (such as a stationery store for example). It definitely would not work for kitchens or cars (whereby the purchase frequency rate is counted in years and not days).

So how can we apply this concept to stores that sell durable goods? Purchases in these stores are not a daily affair like bread, nor do they occur on a weekly or monthly basis. How can we apply this to stores that sell products which are replaced after five or ten years?

There are primarily four ways for stores that sell **durable goods** to develop loyalty.

- **Encourage customers to return** by involving them in events that are not directly or solely business-related (it's the goal of all loyalty or CRM strategies: for example, record the customer's details so he/she can be invited to future events, or call the customer at a later date to check the level of customer satisfaction).
- **Develop supplementary services** that maintain contact with the customer between one purchase and the next (car dealerships also offer a maintenance service through authorised garages; boutiques provide repair services; stores that sell products under warranty sometimes also provide technical support).
- **Add products that consumers use recurrently to the product assortment** (for example, computer stores also sell consumable goods and accessories; stores that sell home appliances also stock spare parts and consumer goods).
- **Try to influence the customer's buying behaviour** to encourage more frequent purchases (for example, leasing agreements are offered to increase the purchase frequency for cars).

Customer satisfaction is a very important key performance indicator: knowing what the customers think about what a store offers enables that store to improve the aspects that the customers believe are the most important. The goal is to increase the probability that the customers will return and speak highly about the store.

The problem with this indicator is that it is rather complex and costly to produce, which is why many stores do not even bother with customer satisfaction.

CUSTOMER SATISFACTION SURVEYS

If you want to know if your customers are satisfied, you need to listen to them and ask for their opinions. There are many different ways to do this, and below I have listed the main ways in ascending order of organisational complexity and level of "intrusion" into the private life of the customer:

1. **Listen to customers** when they spontaneously express an opinion or make a suggestion while in the store;
2. **Gather customer comments and suggestions** by placing a suggestion box in the store;
3. Ask customers to fill in a **short questionnaire** (in the store and preferably on the way out);
4. Ask customers' opinions by **talking to them in the store** (preferably on the way out when the experience is still fresh in their mind);
5. Send a **questionnaire to the customer's home**;
6. **Call customers for a phone interview**.

In all of these methods the main survey tool is the question.
All of these methods fall under the umbrella of customer sat-

isfaction surveys. Before I discuss them in greater detail, I would like to ask you to consider these two questions:

- What is a customer satisfaction indicator for?
- How do we use it?

What does this indicator measure?

A customer satisfaction survey measures the customer's assessment of the shopping experience. By definition it is a *qualitative* indicator as it measures perceptions and opinions rather than hard facts: a positive shopping experience is the result of a complex interplay of sensations, emotions and information that determines whether a customer decides to make a purchase and, even more importantly, return to the store.

We can measure practically every aspect of the customer's experience:

- Product quality and product assortment;
- Price point;
- The quality of the store (aesthetics, cleanliness, temperature, music, first impression, etc.);
- Product displays, easy-to-find products, and comprehensive information about the products;
- Interaction with the sales assistants (understanding of the product, sales techniques, courtesy);
- Standards of service and organisation (for example, queues);
- Overall impression of the experience (was the experience pleasant, what impressions and emotions did the experience arouse?).

Constructing the survey

There are normally four steps to follow when planning a customer satisfaction dashboard:

1. Identify the key areas of focus;
2. Translate these key areas into questions;
3. Decide how you want to collect the information (questionnaire, interview or another method),

4. Define the frequency of the survey:
• Periodic (the survey is carried out once or multiple times a year in a appointed week);
• Continuous (the questionnaire is always available so customers can fill it in whenever they wish).

Repeating the survey

For a customer satisfaction survey to be a useful tool it needs to be repeated over time and/or carried out in multiple stores at the same time. Without a benchmark, no indicator has any real meaning. For example, 97.8% of customers might say that they are satisfied when asked about waiting times at the cash register. This in itself is a high percentage but it can only be interpreted once we have compared it with replies from customers in the previous period or in the chain's other stores. If the average from the other stores, or the result from the previous year, is 98.6%, our information takes on a whole new meaning.

How to use the information

Survey results can be used to:

1. **Identify priority areas** for improvement and implement corrective measures;

2. Summarise the results and **communicate this to the customers**, using the information as a promotional tool;

3. **Discuss the results with the sales staff** and use them for training purposes;

4. Link **part of the staff's variable remuneration** to one or more indicators;

5. Select four to five of the most important questions as "**pillars of customer satisfaction**", track them over time and place emphasis on them on a daily basis.

Let's take a further look at the different ways of gathering customer satisfaction information and analyse the key points.

Method	How	Strengths	Considerations	Costs
Listen to customers in store	• Assemble the sales staff and ask them to take notes each time a customer makes a comment or suggestion. • Collect all the information without being selective. • Cluster the collected information. • Comment on the results during regular meetings.	• Engagement. • All customers are (potentially) heard.	• Requires major involvement of all the staff (the store manager must believe in the method). • Long-term continuity is essential (it cannot be abandoned after a few attempts).	• Staff time.
Suggestion box	• Make a suggestion box with pens and paper available to customers. • Publicise the suggestion box. • Cluster the collected information. • Comment on the results during regular meetings.	• Very cheap and easy to manage. • Not intrusive.	• Not many customers respond. • Once the initial novelty has worn off the box may contain fewer suggestions and only opinions from angry customers and jokes from pranksters.	• Staff time.

Method	How	Strengths	Considerations	Costs
In-store questionnaire	• Make a printed (or touch-screen) questionnaire available to customers by the cash register. • Invite the customer to fill it in (and maybe even offer a small gift). • Regularly process the data.	• Systematic collection of comparable information. • Quick (if the questionnaire is short). • An opportunity to have daily or weekly metrics.	• Cashiers must publicise the system. • Staff might choose which customers they want to do the questionnaire. • Unrepresentative sample: only "willing" customers respond.	• Cost of gifts, if offered. • The time it takes to process the data. • May require software programmes.
In-store interview	• Decide when to collect the data (one week). • Choose customer selection criteria (casual, create a sample based on noticeable characteristics). • Appoint someone (in-house or external) to ask customers if they wish to be interviewed and offer them a small gift in return. • Briefly interview the customer. • Process the results.	• A more representative sample (it is more difficult for the customer to say no). • More accurate and detailed data.	• "Customer satisfaction week" cannot be repeated very often. • Requires the involvement of all the staff.	• The interviewer's cost or time. • Cost of gifts. • The time it takes to process the data.

Method	How	Strengths	Considerations	Costs
Direct Mail questionnaire	• Draw up a list of customers to whom you want to send the questionnaire. • Send the questionnaire to the customers (by post or email). • Await their replies and remind them if they do not reply. • Process the results.	• Systematic collection of comparable information. • Does not involve the store's staff. • Simple process. • An opportunity to have a continuous flow of information (questionnaires sent to all new customers).	• A customer database is required. • The customer may not appreciate the invasion of privacy. • Unrepresentative sample: only "willing" customers respond.	• Postal and IT costs. • The time of the person managing the initiative or the cost of an external agency.
Telephone interview	• Draw up a list of customers and non-customers that you wish to call. • Call the customers and non-customers. • Interview them. • Process the data.	• An opportunity to collect information from non-customers as well (about why they do not use that store). • More accurate and detailed data (if the interviews are carried out properly).	• A customer database is required. • The customer may not appreciate the invasion of privacy. • This may not be managed by in-house staff. • This cannot be repeated very often.	• The cost of an external agency-

MYSTERY SHOPPING

The methods involved with understanding levels of customer satisfaction can often be complicated and limited, so some chains prefer to use a different method that is easier to manage (even though it is not cheaper): mystery shopping. In essence this involves sending a "fake" customer to shop in a store. This customer will have been briefed on which aspects to observe and produces a report after each visit. The report enables the store to assess the quality of service provided based on the shopping experience of that particular "customer". If plenty of visits are made to a store, the information produced with this method can be very reliable, and is often more reliable than information obtained with customer satisfaction surveys.

The main ingredients of this method are:

1. A **detailed list of aspects to observe** (a checklist), with a rating scale so that the various mystery shoppers work within the same guidelines when judging the store;

2. A **team of mystery shoppers** made up of people that match the customer profiles for that store (for example, young mystery shoppers are selected to assess a store for young people, while mystery shoppers who could be parents are sent to children's stores). They are properly briefed about the method and specific checklist beforehand;

3. **Visits are scheduled** for different days of the week and times of the day, to cover both the peak and non-peak periods;

4. **The results are processed** to provide quantitative and qualitative feedback with analytic and concise information (so that the results can be benchmarked against results from different stores and from the same store over a period of time).

Before exploring some of the details of mystery shopping any further, I would like to point out a major difference between this method and customer satisfaction research: customer satisfaction surveys record the perceptions of real customers, thereby enabling a store to understand what they appreciate most and what they find most annoying; the mystery shopper offers a snapshot of maximum and minimum *compliance with an established standard* of service. If a company wishes to employ a mystery shopping service, it first needs to define standards of service, i.e. decide:

• The appearance and ambience of the store (store windows, product presentation, product quantities, standard of cleanliness, temperature, lighting, music, smell, etc.);

• What must happen during the main phases of the shopping experience (the customer enters, walks around, chooses, asks for help, decides to make a purchase, pays, and leaves), i.e. what is the "ideal" interaction between customer and sales assistant.

Standards of service are part of a company's strategy and represent an interpretation of the customer's needs and a promise: it's as if the company is telling its customers, "This is the experience you will have in our stores."

One criticism that is often made about mystery shopping is that it offers poor statistical reliability. The argument is that you cannot judge a store negatively just because a couple of customers during a six-month period were not treated as well as usual. There is some truth to this objection, however it does not place the correct value on the concept of standard of service: if, for example, a store should open at 8.30, and this is a promise that has been made to the customer, the fact that it opens late even once is a violation of the customer's "rights". Mystery shopping forces an organisation to take any promises made to the customer about standards of service seriously, and ensure that they are more thorough in their implementation.

One last question: how can this be used in the store?

1. **Everybody on the sales team must know the standards of service** or at least the checklist with which they are assessed. It is therefore the store manager's responsibility to inform them.

2. The sales staff must be told about these visits and their goals, but naturally **they must not be told when and how often** mystery shoppers visit the store. There are two reasons for this:

- To ensure that they remain more attentive towards customers even when no visits are scheduled;
- To allow the mystery shopper's results to be used at a later date as an opportunity to improve performance.

3. The store manager can use mystery shopping results to evaluate the standard of service provided and **identify areas for improvement**.

4. The sales staff must **have access to the results** in two different yet complementary ways:

- Individually so that they can examine reports of visits that directly concern them;
- Group meetings to discuss the results, celebrate successes, and identify measures to improve performance.

5. The results of the mystery shopper's visits can be viewed as a whole and used to generate a **performance bonus** for everyone that works in the store. Alternatively, they can be used as a way to give a small **individual bonus** or reward to the staff member that received a positive report.

Let's imagine that the twin stores are part of a chain that periodically carries out a customer satisfaction survey to check the standard of service being offered to its customers. Let's also imagine that the company has chosen the answers to five questions as their "pillars" of service:

1. The store is a pleasant place to visit and I feel at home;
2. I always find what I am looking for;
3. The sales assistants are really enthusiastic about the products they sell;
4. Whenever I need information or advice the sales staff have the answers and are delighted to help.
5. I would recommend this store to a friend.

These are the results of this year's survey.

"Pillar of service"	Company average	Store A		Store B	
		Current year	Previous year	Current year	Previous year
A pleasant place	85%	84%	85%	85%	85%
Always find what I want	81%	88%	88%	73%	74%
Enthusiastic about products	96%	88%	88%	97%	89%
Information and advice	93%	75%	85%	95%	94%
I recommend the store	88%	90%	89%	91%	89%

How can you link these to the other KPIs that you already know for the two stores?

_____

_____

_____

_____

What would you do in Store A?

_____

_____

_____

_____

What would you do in Store B?

_____

_____

_____

_____

Now we are going to look at the products, the physical "pieces" that are stocked in a store. Generally speaking, theirs is a fairly easy story to tell:

1. They are selected and added to the product assortment;
2. They are ordered;
3. They arrive at the store;
4. They are put on sale (or temporarily stored "behind the scenes");
5. The customer buys them;
6. They leave the store.

In this chapter we will try to understand, and therefore measure, what happens between steps two and six of this process. In the next chapter we will focus on the products that "get lost" from one step to the next or are "returned to the sender".

First though, a premise and a general rule.

The premise: the quantity of products in a store at any given time is called **stock**, and stock can be measured by volume or by value in three ways:

• (volume) the number of pieces or packages in a store on a certain date;

• (value) the sum of the cost prices of the products in a store on a certain date;

• (value) the sum of the selling prices of the products in a store on a certain date.

The general rule: stock costs money because it is made up of products that have been purchased but not yet sold. So the store's money is tied-up. When talking about stock, we can say that "small is better".

Let's start by looking at our twin stores. We need to analyse what has been ordered and sold in a given period. Let's imagine a situation like this:

	Store A	Store B
No. of pcs in the store (ending inventory from the previous period)	2,500	2,480
No. of new pcs (ordered and arrived)	1,600	1,500
Total no. of pcs available for sale (beginning inventory)	4,100	3,980
No. of pcs sold in this period	1,157	945
No. of pcs remaining at the end of the period (ending inventory)	2,943	3,035

A certain quantity of products remained in the stores on a particular date. Then an order was done, new products arrived and the store filled up again. As time goes by some products are sold and others remain in the warehouse. Products need to be reordered and the cycle begins again.

At this time it is clear that Store B has more stock and has therefore "tied-up" a larger sum of money.

We can illustrate the story of the stock on a graph like this:

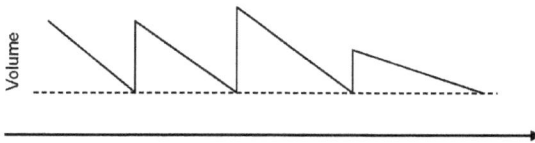

The quantity of products in the store gradually decreases; when it reaches a minimum level, below which the store risks losing sales, a new quantity of products is ordered. The dotted line shows the reorder point.

Given the cost of buying and storing products, it is in the store's interest to handle the smallest possible amount of products. Deciding the quantity of products to stock in a store means finding a balance between two rather conflicting "ideals":

• Stocking plenty of products so I can meet any need a customer may have;

- Stocking only the products that I am sure will sell in the store, without needing to buy even one more product than necessary.

When described like this, these two ideals are clearly unattainable and represent two conflicting goals in constant pressure against each other.

When we want to measure the ability to achieve this delicate balance, we normally use two indicators: turnover and coverage.

INVENTORY TURNOVER

Inventory turnover measures how many times the stock is completely replenished during a given period (the year is normally used as the period of reference). This indicator answers the following question: if I waited until the store was completely empty before ordering new products, how many times would I need to order products to fill the store over the course of a year? Of course, inventory turnover is a theoretical metric because the store is never emptied completely.

What does this indicator measure?

This indicator allows us to measure the ability to order "little and well". High turnover is synonymous with good management.

How do I calculate this indicator?

It can be calculated based on either the number of pieces or in terms of value, which is usually the selling price. Cash register software can provide both these figures because they allow you to "upload" the products when they arrive at the store and then "unload" them when the customer pays and takes them away.

This is the formula:

$$\frac{Total\ sales\ for\ the\ period}{Average\ stock\ for\ the\ period}$$

What is this indicator called in your business?	
Where can you find this data?	
The benchmark for your store	

Let's calculate the turnover rate for the twin stores. Let's suppose that the figures in the previous table represent the average monthly figures and we calculate the turnover for the number of pieces. We need to do two intermediate calculations: calculate the number of pieces sold in the year and calculate the average stock (the mean of the beginning inventory and ending inventory).

The result confirms that Store A is better at managing its stock because it manages to achieve a more rapid turnover:

	Store A	Store B
No. of pcs sold in the year	13.886 (1,157 x 12)	11,340 (945 x 12)
Average stock in the year	3,521.4 (4,100+2,943)/ 2	3,507.5 (3,980+3,035) / 2
Turnover	3.94 times	3.23 times

STOCK COVER DAYS

The stock cover metric indicates for how many days the store can continue to sell using its existing inventory without ordering any new products. Once again this is a purely theoretical indicator because we do not know that the customers would buy exactly what they found in the shop if the store didn't reorder any products.

What does this indicator measure?

This indicator also allows us to measure the ability to order only the bare minimum. But in this case the scale is reversed: a high rate of coverage is synonymous with bad management because it indicates the store has difficulty selling some products, which remain in the warehouse for too long.

How do I calculate this indicator?

It can be calculated based on either the number of pieces or in terms of value, which is usually the selling price, by using this formula:

$$\frac{Average\ stock\ for\ the\ period}{Average\ daily\ sales\ for\ the\ period}$$

What is this indicator called in your business?	

Where can you find this data?	

The benchmark for your store	

Let's calculate the number of stock cover days for our twin stores. Once again we are working on the premise that the figures in the previous table represent the average monthly figures. This time we only need to do one intermediate calculation: calculate the average stock (the mean of the beginning inventory and ending inventory).

The result confirms that Store A is better at managing its stock because it has fewer stock cover days:

	Store A	Store B
Average stock in the year	3,521.4 (4,100+2,943)/ 2	3,507.5 (3,980+3,035)/ 2
Average no. of pcs sold per month	1,157	945
Coverage	67 days	82 days

Which variables influence turnover and coverage?

The size of the inventory, or stock level, is influenced essentially by four important variables:

1. The **choice of products to put on sale** (customers do not buy products if they don't appreciate them; therefore less popular products remain unsold and bump up stock levels);

2. The **ability to present products to best advantage** (customers do not buy products if they cannot find them, if they are not well displayed, or if they appear old, dirty or broken);

3. The **selling price** (customers do not buy products if they think they are too expensive or if they can buy them cheaper elsewhere);

4. The **ability to order the right quantity of products** (so that the store has no surplus stock or products that are becoming obsolete).

What are the store manager's actionable levers?

There is a lot that a store manager can do to ensure proper stock management. In addition to making the right orders (if this lever is available), the store manager can take the follow action:

1. **Supervise the reordering process** to ensure orders are placed with due care. When reordering is delegated to someone else the store manager can teach employees how to reorder and carefully monitor these orders;

2. **Promptly identify products** with insufficient turnover and improve their in-store presentation to increase sales (for example, place them in prominent positions in promotional areas or in the

store window, increase or improve the customer information on the shelves or racks, place the products in higher visibility positions);

3. **Check the selling price is correct** for products with a low turnover and change it if necessary (if, for example, the store across the street is selling the same product at a lower price, sales of that product will probably suffer);

4. **Train sales assistants how to suggest not only products that are popular with customers** (or that they like most), which therefore "sell themselves", but also the products that are more difficult to move;

5. **Targeted use of the promotion lever** to reduce stock levels by adopting "sharp" price cuts as well as discounts on product combinations.

14. THE LINK BETWEEN WHAT COMES IN AND WHAT GOES OUT: DAMAGED ITEMS, SHRINKAGE, AND RETURNS

Let's start with an example.

Imagine a water supply network. The water is taken from a lake, river or underground source, transferred into pipes, and after travelling through the pipes it comes out of the taps in our homes. During its journey a percentage of this water is lost: the pipes have small leaks here and there which generate wastage. Of course it is hoped that as little water as possible leaks from the pipes.

The situation with a store's stock is similar: not all the products purchased by the store end up in the customers' homes; some get lost along the way. So, another way to monitor stock is to check how much of the stock purchased actually arrives in the customers' homes.

Before we go into greater detail I need to introduce three new terms that are commonly used in the retail industry:

• Sell-in (= what comes into the store) is all the products purchased by the store (and therefore sold by suppliers);

• Sell-out (=what goes out of the store) is all the products purchased by the customers (and therefore sold by the store);

• The ratio between these two indicators is known as the sell-through (or "sell-thru"). This indicator measures the ratio (percentage) of goods effectively sold to the total quantity purchased

$$Sell\ through = \frac{Sell\ out}{Sell\ in} \times 100$$

IN-STORE LOGISTICS

Here I have simplified the process but basically the logistics in a store can be described like this:

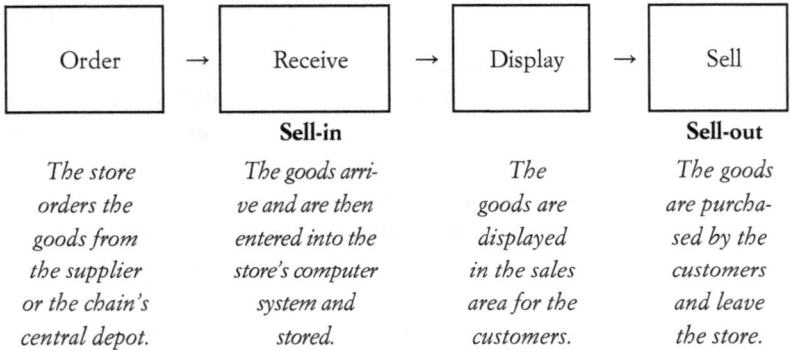

Order	→	Receive	→	Display	→	Sell
		Sell-in				**Sell-out**
The store orders the goods from the supplier or the chain's central depot.		*The goods arrive and are then entered into the store's computer system and stored.*		*The goods are displayed in the sales area for the customers.*		*The goods are purchased by the customers and leave the store.*

"Shrinkages" occur during this process: some products are lost and some are no longer sellable. Let's look at the three main reasons for these losses:

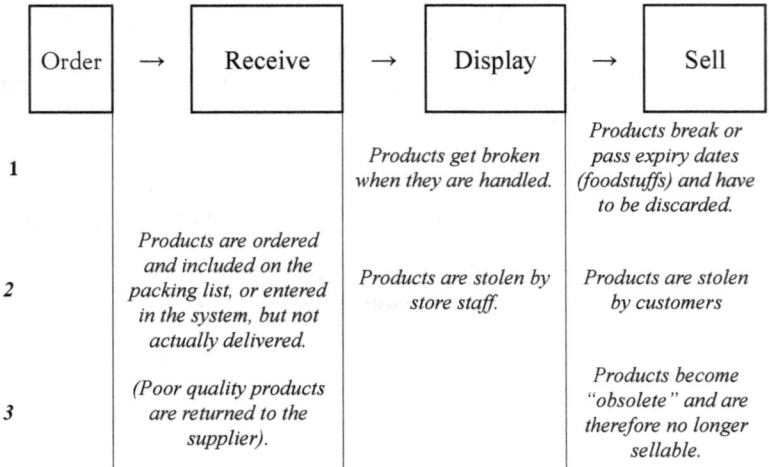

	Order	→	Receive	→	Display	→	Sell
1					*Products get broken when they are handled.*		*Products break or pass expiry dates (foodstuffs) and have to be discarded.*
2			*Products are ordered and included on the packing list, or entered in the system, but not actually delivered.*		*Products are stolen by store staff.*		*Products are stolen by customers*
3			*(Poor quality products are returned to the supplier).*				*Products become "obsolete" and are therefore no longer sellable.*

Row 1 shows the so-called "damaged items": these products are discarded.

Row 2 shows the "shrinkage" items, i.e. the products that

should be at the store (because they were entered into the system upon arrival and have still not been sold), but are not actually there. Shrinkage refers to inventory differences. Each store always has a "theoretical" book inventory that sums all the products that have arrived and been entered into the system; all products that leave the store via the cash registers are then subtracted from this amount. A physical stock check is also carried out with an established pattern of regularity (every month or every three or six months depending on the goods and the procedures of the store or chain), and all products actually in the store are physically counted. There is always a difference between these two inventories: some products that should be in the store in reality are not there. If a store keeps records of the damaged items, the difference between the two inventories can mainly be traced to theft or to administrative errors when inputting the data.

Row 3 shows the products that should be returned to the supplier because they are no longer sellable. Whether or not the store can actually return the goods (to the supplier or to the central depot) depends on company rules or on the agreement with the suppliers. Whatever the case, the returns indicator measures a failure by the store, which has purchased a product believing that it will sell it but has failed to do so. If returns are discarded, they come under the first category (even if they are not damaged or broken); otherwise they are managed with a different procedure and therefore with a different indicator. These are products that are no longer "good" and are often transferred into a different sales channel so that they may be sold.

There is also a second category for returns. These products are returned due to poor quality but this is normally guaranteed by the supplier and so we will not cover this in this chapter (even though poor quality shipments can affect the store, which finds itself without goods when it needs them.

These are the results for the twin stores:

	Store A	Store B	Company average
Shrinkage	1.17%	0.80%	1.05%
Damaged items	0.99%	0.60%	0.75%
Returns	3.50%	6.70%	4.00%

How would you interpret this data?

_____

_____

_____

_____

Now let's have a detailed look at the three indicators.

DAMAGED ITEMS

These are all the products that deteriorate during the logistics process at the store and need to be removed from sale. These products are discarded basically for two reasons: because they break or because they pass their expiry date.

What does this indicator measure?

The number and value of the products that get discarded. This represents a significant loss of margin for the store.

The indicator measures the care with which goods are handled within the store: many damaged items can actually be avoided by taking greater care over how the work is carried out.

How do I calculate this indicator?

There is no automatic system to track damaged and broken items. To obtain this information you need a procedure in which every piece is tracked and "unloaded" by the system before being discarded.

Two different methods can be used to calculate the value of discarded and damaged items: the cost price and the selling price.

The first (cost price) is more correct for accounting purposes and is the methods used in the profit and loss statement (see Chapter 17): the store incurs a loss that is limited to the amount spent to purchase the product which is later discarded.

The second (selling price) is more useful from a commercial perspective because it measures the value of the lost sale (the lost opportunity) and takes into account the fact that, in addition to cost price, the item also consumed other resources, such as space and the staff's time, before it was discarded.

These are the formulae:

Volume = sum of the discarded pieces

Value = sum of the (cost or selling) prices of discarded pieces

$$Percentage = \frac{Number / Value\ of\ discarded\ pieces \times 100}{Total\ sales\ (no.\ of\ pieces\ or\ value)}$$

What is this indicator called in your business?	

Where can you find this data?	

The benchmark for your store	

Which variables influence the indicator?

The amount of damaged items basically depends on two variables:

1. **Purchasing excessive quantities of goods** (in the case of foodstuffs the main cause of damage is the product passing its "best before" date; another factor is that a packed warehouse is more difficult to manage);

2. **How the product is managed** (the care and attention taken by staff when handling the goods).

Which actionable levers can the store manager use to change the indicator?

To keep this indicator in check, the store manager must make sure that **ordering is organised to best advantage** and that **the staff "treat the goods with care" every step of the way**, particularly:

- When unpacking the goods;
- When storing the goods;
- When stocking shelves or displaying the goods;
- When selling the goods;
- When cleaning the store.

SHRINKAGE

This indicator measures the difference (pieces or value) between the book inventory and the physical inventory.

What does this indicator measure?

This indicator measures the quantity and the value of products that "disappear" from the store. Sometimes damaged and broken items are also included in shrinkage (if these have not been tracked by a separate system); otherwise this indicator measures solely theft and unidentified administrative errors. In both cases these products have been purchased but have not been sold, returned or discarded.

How do I calculate this indicator?

Once the physical stock check has been completed, we need to attribute a value to the missing products using the selling price applied on the day on which they were inventoried. The sum of these amounts gives us the shrinkage value. The number of pieces is not particularly interesting but is easy to obtain. These are the formulae:

$$Volume = number\ of\ disappeared\ pieces$$

$$Value = sum\ of\ the\ (cost\ or\ selling)\ prices\ of\ disappeared\ products$$

$$Percentage = \frac{Sum\ of\ the\ (cost\ or\ selling)\ prices\ of\ disappeared\ products}{Total\ sales} \times 100$$

With regard to the criteria for determining the value, the same considerations made for the damaged items apply here.

What is this indicator called in your business?	*[handwritten]*

Where can you find this data?	*[handwritten]*

The benchmark for your store	*[handwritten]*

Which variables influence the indicator?

Shrinkage is caused by **errors or theft and these are attributable to three main players in the commercial chain**:

1. The people that deliver the goods to the store;
2. The people that work in the store;
3. The customers.

Which actionable levers can the store manager use to change the indicator?

The main actionable lever at the store manager's disposal is **controlling** the three "players".

1. With regard to whoever delivers the goods it is vital that somebody checks that **the order, what is written on the delivery notes and what is actually delivered all match perfectly**. This difference is often simply due to an error at the distribution centre when preparing the goods and somebody makes a mistake when loading the delivery truck. However, once the goods have been accepted, any differences become the store's responsibility.

2. The store manager has three possible lines of action with regard to the **staff**:

• Establish and implement a **procedure for carrying out checks** (for example, stores that sell luxury goods may carry out searches at the end of the day);

   • **Set an example** (be the first the comply with procedure) and follow it to the letter;

   • **Monitor the situation** carefully and when you suspect somebody act firmly but with discretion;

   • Call the police if a problem arises.

   3. The following action can be taken with regard to the **customers**:

   • **Protect valuable goods** using anti-shoplifting methods (for example, video cameras, tags or other electronic article surveillance and identification systems);

   • Establish a **procedure for carrying out checks** that does not entail "taking the law into your own hands", but still deters the customer from "having a go";

   • **Raise the staff's awareness** about the importance and the sensitivity of this subject so that they can recognise and report and suspicious behaviour;

   • **Call the police** if a problem arises.

RETURNS

A return is a product that is returned to the supplier or to the warehouse because:
- **It was not sold within a certain period of time;**
- **It was unsuccessfully offered at a discounted price.**

Goods may only be returned if the procedure is provided for by an agreement between the store and the supplier (independent stores) or by in-house regulations (chain stores with central management).

If a store does not have the possibility to return goods to the supplier, any products that are no longer sellable will be discounted multiple times and then either discarded or sold in lots to stockists, which move them through other channels (for example, outlets, street markets or export.). If goods are sold to stockists, they will be recorded as a loss only for the difference between the cost price and the amount paid by the stockist.

What does this indicator measure?

The concept of returns mostly applies to non-food products (although this is not a hard and fast rule), which are not perishable, but are still subject to "obsolescence": they become obsolete because they go out of fashion or are superseded by more modern products. Returns also figure in product categories that operate by "collection" or season, such as apparel.

A certain percentage of returns is only normal: if a store wants to offer a complete product assortment, it needs to purchase a little more than it will sell. So, the indicator measures the ability to "guess" the order and the ability to sell most of the available product assortment.

How do I calculate this indicator?

These are the commonly used formulae:

$$Volume = number\ of\ returned\ products$$

$$Value = sum\ of\ the\ cost\ prices\ of\ returned\ products$$

$$Percentage = \frac{Sum\ of\ the\ cost\ prices\ of\ returned\ products}{Total\ sales} \times 100$$

Another method used to calculate the percentage is this:

$$\frac{(Sell\ in - Sell\ out)}{Sell\ out} \times 100$$

When using this formula, damaged items and shrinkage must first be deducted from the sell-out for the data to be reliable.

What is this indicator called in your business?	

Where can you find this data?	

The benchmark for your store	

Which variables influence the indicator?

This indicator essentially measures the **quality**:

• **Of the purchase process;**
• **Of the sales process.**

Which actionable levers can the store manager use to change the indicator?

The store manager can take the same actions listed in the previous chapter that refer to stock cover to optimise the management of returned goods:

1. Check the **ordering** process;

2. **Identify as soon as possible any products** that the customer tends not to buy and try to emphasise them using merchandising techniques;

3. Check the **selling price**;

4. Work with the sales assistants to identify **sales arguments and methods to sell products** that are less popular with the customers;

5. Use the **promotion lever**.

This is the situation of the personnel costs in the two stores:

	Store A	Store B	Company average
Total personnel costs	2,430	2,570	
Incidence on sales	15%	17%	14.60%
Sales per hour	81	75.60	85.01

How would you interpret this data?

_____

_____

_____

_____

There are two parameters we normally use to help us to understand how and how much a store spends on personnel:
• The sum of the staff's wages, in absolute value, compared with the total sales;
• Sales per hour, i.e. the ratio of sales to the sum of hours worked.

Let's analyse them one by one.

PERSONNEL COSTS

This figure is the total costs incurred by the store to pay for the work performed by all the staff (store manager, sales assistants, cashiers, visual, warehouse operatives, stock keepers, supervisors, etc.).

What does this indicator measure?

It measures the combined sum of the staff's wages, which are structured in different ways according to types of employment contracts and national legislations. Generally speaking, we can say that staff wages comprise:

• Some fixed amounts that are not linked to the employee's results (pay + the taxes and contributions that the employer pays to the state and to social security institutions);

• Some variable amounts which are performance-related (such as, end-of-year bonuses or commissions on sales made by the individual sales assistant).

How do I calculate these indicators?

When adding up the personnel costs we need to take into account every type of cost, even those that the employee does not see (such as, social security contributions for example). Payroll data are usually managed by a different software programme than the one used for sales so this indicator is often compiled manually or with a separate procedure; in many companies this information is produced by the head office.

These are the formulae:

$$Value = sum\ of\ the\ personnel\ costs$$

$$Percentage = \frac{Personnel\ costs}{Sales} \times 100$$

What is this indicator called in your business?	

Where can you find this data?	

The benchmark for your store	

Which variables influence the indicator?

The personnel costs incurred by a store can be divided into two macro components: the **average hourly cost** (how much the staff are paid on average) and the **sum of hours worked** in a given period of time.

The average hourly cost can only be partially influenced by the employer. It depends on:

1. The average level of **wages** in that period, sector and job market;

2. The type of **employment contract** (each country has different types of contract with different conditions and costs to the employer);

3. The **pay policy** (each employer can decide to pay its staff more or less, providing that it complies with the national minimum wage that the workers are entitled to by law);

4. **Length of service in the company** (employees with a longer service record are normally paid more than someone who has been there for a shorter period for doing the same job);

5. The **merit pay policy** (each employer can choose whether to pay undifferentiated wages, or to pay performance–related wages which may vary considerably);

6. The incidence of **overtime** (which usually has a higher pay rate than normal working hours) on the total hours worked.

The sum of hours worked depends on:

- **How many people work in a store** (staff);
- **How many hours they actually work per week** in total and individually (full time or part time, including overtime and less holidays and sick leave).

This second figure influences the sales per hour, which we will discuss later.

What are the store manager's actionable levers?

The store manager is responsible for the store's results so his or her goal is to have a team that works well but also to control the personnel costs. The following tips are consistent with the second objective; we should not forget though that some of the solutions may impact negatively on the quality of service and staff's remuneration. They should therefore be implemented together with some "antidotes", which I have included in brackets.

To lower personnel costs the store manager can:

1. **Select staff carefully** so that the personnel in the store are motivated to do their jobs;

2. Select **inexperienced people** (in this case you need to factor in the time required to train these people);

3. Adopt **employment contracts that are cost-effective for the employer** (with the risk that people will leave as soon as they find a better paid job or one that offers greater security);

4. **Plan shifts** to match busy and quiet periods; if staff are only in the store when they are needed, you can reduce those periods when the sales assistants are being paid even though they have nothing productive to do;

5. Establish **efficient working methods** so staff are not performing unnecessary activities, and reduce the amount of paperwork;

6. **Supervise the shifts** and the work that needs to be done so that you can reduce the amount of overtime to the bare minimum;

7. **Always be in the store** ("on the floor"), together with the people, and set an example;

8. **Introduce performance-related pay** to motivate the sales assistants to work harder (this choice does not reduce the amount of the personnel costs, but it does affect their impact on sales);

9. **Monitor absenteeism** (constant sick leave close to other holidays) **and "slack" time** (start and finish work punctually, respect coffee and lunch breaks), and take firm action if staff conduct does not comply with the rules.

SALES PER HOUR

In a given period, sales per hour is the ratio of the store's turnover (sales) to the sum of hours that had to be worked to produce those sales.

What does this indicator measure?

The average productivity in one hour of work in that store, i.e. how many sales does one hour of work generate on average.

As with all productivity indicators, sales per hour can be used to take stock of a situation and check what has happened, or as a preventive tool to establish how many hours are required to meet a given sales forecast.

How do I calculate this indicator?

The sum of hours worked is usually produced by a different software programme than the one used for sales; therefore the indicator is often compiled manually or with a separate procedure.

This is the formula:

$$\frac{Sales}{Number\ of\ hours\ worked}$$

What is this indicator called in your business?	
Where can you find this data?	
The benchmark for your store	

How to set a productivity goal

Once the store manager has a set of sales forecast and a standard of sales per hour, he or she can establish the number of labour hours required. Afterwards the figures can be checked to see if the store met the forecast.

To establish the standard of productivity, you need to be very well acquainted with your business and decide which standard of service you want to provide. For example, if the store manager decides that only one person instead of two is needed on the second floor on Wednesdays, the productivity of that floor on that day will be doubled. This only works though if we presume that the absence of a second sales assistant does not cause poor service or any lost sales (for example, some customers might have to wait too long to be served, get fed up and leave without buying anything) and it must not have a negative impact on the turnover.

Of course, the store manager is never completely free to organise the shifts exactly as he or she pleases because the conditions set by employment contracts must be taken into consideration (minimum and maximum hours per day, working hours, breaks, holidays, national or bank holidays, etc.).

Which variables influence the indicator?

The sales per hour figure is influenced by:
• **The products sold by the store**;
• **The average selling price**;
• **The standard of service** (self-service or full-service);
• A customers **"willingness"** (if the customer is willing to wait, you can work with a higher rate of productivity);
• The efficacy and efficiency of **in-house working procedures**;
• The staff's average **skill** level;
• **Flexible working hours**;
• **Motivation** and average level of staff diligence ("speed" and flexibility).

Sales per hour is not influenced by the type of employment contract or by the average hourly cost; this means that it allows for an easier comparison between situations even with very different personnel unit costs.

What are the store manager's actionable levers?

The same suggestions given for the average hourly cost can

also be applied to the sales per hour indicator. I think it is important to underline this concept though: to improve productivity, the store manager needs to act shrewdly to improve the way in which things are done in the store and, at the same time, to ensure that staff are always attentive towards customers. If the store manager fails in this, any savings made with the sales per hour indicator will probably have a negative impact on sales.

SALES PER FTE

Another way to calculate staff productivity rate is to measure the annual sales per FTE (full-time equivalent), i.e. the level of productivity achieved in that store by a full-time employee over the course of a year. We use the term full-time "equivalent" because the store's employees may well have very different and not easily comparable employment contracts. If, for example, a store has a full-time employee, a part-time at 50% employee and a part-time at 70% employee, we can say that 2.2 FTEs work in that store (100% + 50% + 70% = 220%).

The formula is similar to the one used to calculate the sales per hour: divide the annual sales by the number of FTEs that worked on average in that store during the year. This formula is helpful for providing an overall assessment of the productivity levels of a store's staff, or for establishing how many people will be required in a new store before it actually opens based on the forecasted sales; it does not provide any information about day-to-day operations though.

For a store to be operational it will have to incur operating costs in addition to personnel costs: these are the costs involved with actually having and operating the store. These costs are normally dealt with by the store manager.

Operating costs are all the costs relating to the "walls" of the store. These are direct costs that the store has to pay because without them it could neither exist nor operate.

Even though the store manager is responsible for paying these costs, he or she usually only has a significant impact on just a few of them.

What does this indicator measure?
All the costs relating to:
• Payment of rent &/or condominium fees
• The purchase of materials;
• The purchase or depreciation of equipment;
• Utilities (electricity, gas, telephone);
• Cleaning;
• Maintenance;
• Municipal taxes (store windows, rubbish collection, etc.).

How do I calculate this indicator?
Add all the costs together. Normally this figure is also compared as a percentage in relation to the total sales (so it gives you a benchmark against other stores).

What is this indicator called in your business?	

Where can you find this data?	

The benchmark for your store	

Which variables influence the indicator?

The operating costs are for the most part **influenced by the market**:

• The rent will depend on the property values in the area where the store is situated;

• The utilities are set by a regulated market;

• The costs for materials, cleaning and maintenance can be negotiated with the suppliers;

• The municipal taxes are set by the local authorities.

Which actionable levers can the store manager use to change the indicator?

The store manager can influence these costs by **making the staff aware of their existence and by monitoring wastage**. The main areas to keep an eye on are:

• The use of the utilities (lights left on unnecessarily, telephone calls);

• Correct use of the equipment (which reduces the need for maintenance);

• Consumables (for example, bags and wrapping paper);

• Cleaning.

These are the figures for the twin stores. What is your impression of these results?

	Store A	Store B	Company average
Operating costs	800	900	
Incidence on sales	4.94%	5.95%	5.02%

What do you think may have caused this difference?

_____

_____

_____

_____

We have come to the end of our journey of discovery into the world of KPIs for retail. To sum up, I would like to show you a document that gives us an overview of a store's results: the profit and loss statement.

The logic behind this document is relatively simple: you start with the sales and then gradually deduct all the costs that the business has to incur to generate those sales. Every now and then we add up the figures to get our interim margins that help us to measure different aspects that have contributed to the end result. The number at the bottom of the page (the last margin when there are no other costs left to pay, no more investments to amortise, and no taxes to pay) finally tells us how much profit the store has generated.

Sometime we have to add rather than subtract: this is what happens with manufacturer promotions, i.e. when the supplier offers a discount for high-volume orders or for promotions, and when we have financial gains generated by the way we manage the business (such as, the time difference between when the customers pay us and when we pay the suppliers, so they are the result of good inventory turnover).

The profit and loss statement is a very helpful tool in the retail world because it provides an overall view of the store's situation at a glance, which is the fundamental profit centre in this business.

The store manager can trust the profit and loss statement because the first line shows the takings and we know this is a reliable figure: given that all the customers pay immediately (in cash or by credit card, or with payment methods that are sound in the vast majority of cases), the risk of customers not paying is extremely limited and so there are no problems with financing or managing any insolvencies. In terms of other business activities, the profit and loss statement can sometimes be misleading because it can give the impression that money has been collected when this is not actually the case (and perhaps never will be). Therefore, it may offer a snapshot of a profitable business while things are actually going in a completely different direction.

There are different ways to organise a profit and loss statement. The profit and loss statement I have provided here is typical of a store, and you can compare it with the one used by your business by filling in the right-hand column.

Only the costs incurred to purchase the goods that were actually sold during the applicable period are recorded in the profit and loss statement; the cost of purchasing the goods that are still in the store and not bought by the customers (the stock) is not recorded, unless indirectly under "financing costs". The cost of purchasing "lost" products (damaged items, shrinkage and returns) is recorded separately because it does not come under "cost of goods sold" as these products did not leave the store via the cash register.

		Term used in my store:
	Gross sales	
-	VAT	
=	Net sales	
-	Cost of goods sold	
=	*First margin*	
+	Manufacturer promotions	
+	End-of-year bonuses	
=	*Second margin*	
-	Damaged items	
-	Shrinkage	
-	Returns	
=	*Third margin*	
-	Personnel costs	
-	Direct operating costs	
=	*Fourth margin*	
-	Financing costs	
+	Financial profits	
=	*Fifth margin*	

And now we can return to our twin stores for one last time.

By drawing up their profit and loss statements, we can evaluate the overall result of how the two stores were managed. I have left the rows for the manufacturer promotions and the financial costs and profits blank as we have only briefly discussed about these in the book.

		Store A		Store B	
		Absolute values	%	Absolute values	%
Gross sales		19,440.00	120.00%	18,144.00	120.00%
VAT	-	3,240.00	20.00%	3,024.00	20.00%
Net sales		16,200.00	100.00%	15,120.00	100.00%
(Promotions)		*2,997.00*	*18.50%*	*2,026.08*	*13.40%*
Cost of goods sold	-	9,963.00	61.50%	8,920,80	59.00%
First margin		6,237.00	38.50%	6,199,20	41.00%
Manufacturer promotions	+				
End-of-year bonuses	+				
Second margin					
Damaged items	-	160.38	0.99%	90.72	0.60%
Shrinkage	-	189.54	1.17%	120.96	0.80%
Returns	-	567.00	3.50%	1,013.04	6.70%
Third margin		5,320.08	32.84%	4,974.48	32.90%
Personnel	-	2,430.00	15.00%	2,570.40	17.00%
Direct operating costs	-	800.00	4.94%	900.00	5.95%
Fourth margin		2,090.08	12.90%	1,504.08	9.95%
Financing costs	-				
Financial profits	+				
Fifth margin					

What are your final thoughts about how Store A has been managed?

_____

_____

_____

_____

What are your final thoughts about how Store B has been managed?

_____

_____

_____

_____

FOOTFALL

As we have no other information about the two stores, I will suggest some hypotheses that could explain why Store A has a higher footfall:
- It is in a better location;
- It is in a city that has organised events which attracted a lot of people in that period;
- It has better public transport links nearby;
- It has a car park;
- It has better store windows with a tantalising preview of what's inside that tempts customers through the door;
- It keeps the doors open;
- There are no sales assistants at the entrance that discourage customers from entering (or conversely, a very persuasive sales assistant at the door invites customers to come in);
- The staff are very welcoming (positive word of mouth);
- It ran a lot of promotions during that period;
- It has just been refurbished and has a new image that is generating a great deal of curiosity.

As to Store B, in addition to the opposite of the above-mentioned hypotheses, we could also add these:

- Its people-counting system is broken;
- There was really bad weather during this period;
- Roadwork significantly restrict access to the store;
- Everyone knows that it is very expensive, or that you can never find what you want;
- It hasn't been open very long.

NUMBER OF TRANSACTIONS AND CONVERSION RATE

Some hypotheses about the results for Store B:
- It never experiences stock-out (customers always find what they are looking for);
- The sales assistants have more time to dedicate to the customers;
- The sales assistants are more competent;
- Overall the store has an outstanding image (product presentation, electricity, cleaning, etc.)
- It has a high percentage of loyal customers that know what they want when they enter the store.

In addition to the opposite of the above-mentioned hypotheses, the following might be true about Store A:
- The store is too crowded, the sales assistants cannot serve all the customers and inevitably some leaving without buying anything;
- The sales assistants dedicate a great deal of time to the customer that they are serving, and neglect any other customers that may be waiting;
- The prices are higher;
- Many stock-outs (customers do not find what they are looking for);
- A lot of customers come into the store just to browse and have no intention of buying anything.

SALES AND SALES PER SQUARE METRE

Store A has the same number of transactions but the sales results are better. This means that on average every customer spends more money. We do not know why yet. Here a couple of hypotheses:
- The prices are higher (customers buy the same things that they buy in the other store but pay more for them);
- It is situated in an area with a good deal of passing trade so it is normal for lots of people to come in just to browse; those who

come in with "real" intentions of buying something are served attentively.

And a couple of hypotheses for Store B:
• It has very low prices, and focuses on promotions;
• Its sales assistants are very effective; they successfully engage the few customers that come in and complete their sales.

LIKE-FOR-LIKE COMPARISONS

Store A is on the decline, while Store B is going from strength to strength. What are the reasons for these different trajectories?
Store A might be:
• Old and unattractive;
• Tired and at the end of its life cycle;
• Poorly managed;
• Employing demotivated sales assistants;
• Badly hit by the competition;
• Penalised by the fact the offices of a major multinational, which were opposite the store, have moved to another neighbourhood and left the building vacant;
• …

And instead Store B might be:
• New;
• Recently opened;
• Managed by a store manager with a great deal of initiative;
• In a recently built neighbourhood where lots of new families are moving in;
• …

BENCHMARKING

Footfall: Store A is reaching saturation point; Store B still has a chance for improvement.

Number of transactions: both stores have below average results.

Conversion rate: this is Store A's weakness.

BUDGET

The two budgets tell two completely different stories. I'm going to suggest one possible way to interpret the stories by focusing in particular on the possible characteristics of the people who work in the two stores.

First budget: Store A +, Store B -

A is a store in decline. With that diminishing budget, the company knows that there is only so much it can do (perhaps because new stores have opened nearby, putting the store in a difficult position). But despite this, the store is still in business. The store manager has given the sales assistants strict instructions, "You have to forget about those who are just here to browse, and focus on those who will actually buy something. Better to have fewer but better customers!"

Growth is forecast for Store B because it still has potential for development. But B does not keep its promises: it attracts few customers. Those who come, buy: the sales assistants are good at their jobs. But there are still too few customers.

Second budget: Store A -, Store B +

Store A is resting on its successes and does not feel the need to increase the conversion rate: the average sale per transaction is in line with the forecasts, but you cannot say the same about the number of transactions. The sales assistants are satisfied and have no interest in "harassing the customer". They are good at selling but are also losing customers; perhaps they focus too much on old customers and not enough on the new ones.

In Store B though the sales assistants are more proactive, the staff are younger and the mindset is that all the customers can buy something so you need to "have a go with everyone". This is the approach they have decided to use to increase the conversion rate.

The company had not expected the staff working in Store B to be so competent and motivated, or that the market would respond so quickly, and had therefore underestimated the situation.

AVERAGE SELLING PRICE AND UNITS PER TRANSACTION

The simplest explanation for the different results is this: Store B is more expensive and therefore the customers purchase fewer items. Other possible explanations:

- Store A offers more promotions and more discounts;
- Store A mostly sells products and categories that have a lower average price;
- Store A has a better display that encourages impulse purchase;
- Store B is strong in the mid-high price categories on which it has a low-price policy;
- Store B mostly sells more expensive products;
- Store A's sales assistants are more skilled at cross-selling;
- Store B puts together a lot of combined offers.

SALES PER CATEGORY

Store B is more expensive in all the product categories and/or resorts less to using the promotion lever. It is very strong in category 3, which has the highest average price. Its sales assistants are capable of making a quality sale and justifying the price; however this seems to have a detrimental effect on volume.

A question for Store A: how can sales in category 3 be increased? For example, how can you maximise the ability to sell more of what the store already has, steering sales towards category 3?

A question for Store B: how can the volume of other categories be increased, leveraging the sales skills that the sales assistants have already demonstrated?

CROSS-SELLING

Store A sells multiple products to the same customer, but in the same product category; Store B sells fewer but has developed better cross-selling skills. The two stores are in line with each other in terms of penetration of the three categories, except for category 3, in which A is notably lower.

Based on the new information at our disposal, we can refine the two questions from the previous paragraph.

A question for Store A: how can the sales in category 3 be increased? For example, how can you gear the ability to sell more of what the store already has towards different categories?

A question for Store B: how can the average units per transaction be increased, by leveraging the cross-selling skills that the sales assistants have already demonstrated?

MARGINS

If we imagine that the two stores purchase their products with the same terms, the main hypotheses to explore in order to explain the different results of the first margin are:

• Store A has a generally lower price line (the same product is cheaper in Store A than in Store B);

• Store A sells a larger quantity of products using promotions (so its customers often buy discounted or promotion products);

• Store A's customers favour products at lower prices within the commercial offering; despite operating with the same selling prices, the margin mix is lower because a Store A customer mainly chooses the cheaper products in the various product categories.

PERCENTAGE OF REVENUE FROM PROMOTIONS

The hypothesis that Store B does not make enough use of the promotion lever has been confirmed, particularly for categories 1 and 2 (the ones in which it does not excel). Given that its main goal is to increase volume, it could make better use of this lever (it could improve by approximately 3%).

Store A still has room to develop promotional policies aimed at increasing the sales for category 3, in which it invests little.

CUSTOMER SATISFACTION

The results show several leads that warrant further investigation:

• The products in Store A are well managed (customers find what they are looking for), but the support provided by sales assistants to customers during the purchasing phase has weakened;

• Store B shows a marked improvement in terms of the ability of its sales assistants, but has problems when it comes to displaying and managing the products (customers do not find what they are looking for).

This information can be linked to the observations made about the footfall, conversion rate, and average sale per transaction. Another area to explore is how the goods are managed (Chapters 14 and 15).

DAMAGED ITEMS, SHRINKAGE, RETURNS

The new information gives us a better understanding of what is happening in the two stores, and also enables us to better interpret the customer satisfaction results:

• Store A is less careful about how the goods are managed and handled and therefore has more damaged items and thefts. However, it is better at managing the orders and clearing its stock (using targeted promotion policies);

• Store B looks after its goods but buys too much stock and not the right products (i.e. it does not buy what the customer needs). Furthermore, it does not pay enough attention to clearing its stock.

PERSONNEL COSTS AND SALES PER HOUR

Store A has fewer people or people that are younger on average. Store B has a greater number of resources at its disposal but this does not translate into additional sales. Perhaps the staff are aiming for higher sales which the store does not expand upon.

Both stores have higher costs than the company average; reducing the impact of personnel costs could be a priority for both of them.

OPERATING COSTS

We can only make a few hypotheses as we do not have detailed information about the costs:

• Store B has opened only recently and pays a higher rent;

• Store A is very careful about saving money (consumables, utilities, and generally pays more attention to the store which cuts down on extra costs for cleaning and maintenance companies), while Store B on the other hand is not particularly conscientious about this aspect;

• Store A has negotiated better terms with the cleaning company and the maintenance providers;

• Store B is older and constantly requires extra maintenance and repairs.

SUMMARY: THE PROFIT AND LOSS STATEMENT

Store A produces a higher margin in both absolute and relative value. It shows better stock and cost management and a greater capacity for generating sales volumes.

Store B produces lower volumes, with higher profit margins, but its ineffective management of the stock and direct costs is compromising its results.

A possible area of focus for store manager A: increase sales to reverse the downward trend.

A possible area of focus for store manager B: pay greater attention to the way the inventory turnover (make reordering and promotional choices a priority) and costs in general are managed.